THUNDERBIRD
Milestones

Mike Mueller

MBI Publishing Company

First published in 1999 by MBI Publishing Company, PO Box 1, 729 Prospect Avenue, Osceola, WI 54020-0001 USA

MBI Publishing Company books are also available at discounts in bulk quantity for industrial or sales-promotional use. For details write to Special Sales Manager at Motorbooks International Wholesalers & Distributors, 729 Prospect Avenue, PO Box 1, Osceola, WI 54020-0001 USA.

Library of Congress Cataloging-in-Publication Data

Mueller, Mike
    Thunderbird milestones / Mike Mueller
        p. cm. -- (Enthusiast color series)
    Includes index.
    ISBN 0-7603-0474-2 (pbk. : alk. paper)
    1. Thunderbird automobile--History. I. Title.
II. Series.
TL215.T46M84 1999
629.222'2--dc21

On the front cover: In the Kennedy and Eisenhower years, nothing satisfied the driving public's desire for personal luxury and style like the Thunderbird. These models are often cited as the top form of the marque – a 1957 in front backed by a 1960 (left) and 1963 Sports Roadster. The '57 is owned by Richard and Kathey Goodroe of Annistown, Georgia; the '60 is owned by Tom Schirra of Marietta, Georgia; and the '63 Sports Roadster is owned by Alton Maxwell of Tucker, Georgia.

On the frontispiece: Few parts of the Thunderbird's gilding convey its spirit and style like the rear trunkplate on the 1957 model.

On the title page: As the height of aerodynamic design for their respective eras, the 1997 Thunderbird and the 1957 Thunderbird look right at home amid the warbirds of the Fantasy of Flight Aviation Museum in Florida. The '57 T-Bird is owned by Don and Pat Petrus of Winter Haven, Florida.

On the back cover: The beginning and end of an era – the red 1997 Thunderbird was the last off the Ford assembly line and the black 1955 T-Bird is recognized as the oldest in existence. It carries serial number 005. The '55 T-Bird is owned by George Watts of Orange, California.

Edited by Christopher Batio
Designed by Dan Perry

Printed in Hong Kong

Contents

Acknowledgments

Most questions concerning the T-Bird's revival will likely have been answered by the time you turn this page. What was the future for this humble scribe in 1998 is now late-breaking news for anyone within eyeshot of these words. So it is left to these 96 pages to remind you—and hopefully a few gazillion other readers—of the rich Thunderbird heritage that came before. It is lucky for all of us that so many devoted T-Bird fans have been so eager over the years to preserve that heritage. Lucky for me, too. Without the enthusiastic assistance of so many wonderfully energetic 'Bird watchers, this effort would have never taken flight.

First and foremost I must mention my good friend Max Dilley back home in Urbana, Illinois. Max and I originally crossed paths about five years back when I was working on a Mustang book, and he was still heavily involved in pony-car collecting. His easygoing enthusiasm made those first photo shoots no sweat, just fun and friendly. Max not only opened his garage for me, he opened his home. In the years since he has also never failed to answer the phone with a warm and welcoming "can do," just as he did in December 1997 when I came calling with a last-minute photo request involving his beautiful blue 1957 'Bird.

On short notice, and with less-than-desirable weather conditions making for a miserable Midwestern morning, Max came through yet again, driving his T-Bird some 15 miles despite the threat of rain. Or maybe even snow. Only after the shoot had been scheduled did I learn that his mother, Ruth Dilley, had passed away just the week before. I felt pretty small, but Max wouldn't let me feel bad, nor would he let me down. Life apparently does go on, as does my belief that I just may be one of the luckiest guys on the planet for having friends like Max Dilley.

Ray Quinlan is another friend who has also bent over backwards for me time and again whenever I've passed through Champaign, Illinois, looking for a helping hand. I would also like to thank my brother, Dave Mueller, who has always been there for me—on photo shoots or otherwise; my brother-in-law, Frank Young, who works so cheap it almost makes me feel guilty—almost; another brother, Jim Mueller Jr., and my father, Jim Sr., both also never shy about dropping everything when I come demanding. Last, but in no way least, is my very best friend, Joyce Tucker, who continually amazes me with her energy as well as her selflessness. You go, girl—and take me with you.

Glorious Thunderbird memories have been preserved for the ages thanks to enthusiasts like Max Dilley, shown here applying some TLC to his 1957 'Bird in front of his Urbana, Illinois, home.

Then there are all the club people whose friendly support was also greatly appreciated: Harvey Hodges in Champaign, Illinois; Jim Hack and George Watts of the Classic Thunderbird Club International in Signal Hill, California; Ken Leaman and Malcolm Green in New Jersey; Dr. Richard Schatz of the International Thunderbird Club in Sugarloaf, Pennsylvania; Richard and Kathy Goodroe, Elton Roberts, and Alton Maxwell, all of the Atlanta Classic Thunderbird Club.

Kudos go as well to Gil Baumgartner and Eric Larson. Baumgartner, a renowned Thunderbird restoration expert from Suisun, California, made 15 minutes of fame possible with Bo Cheadle's fabulous 1957 Battlebird. Great job, Gil, and thanks so much for your patience. Larson, curator of the Octave Chanute Aerospace Museum in Rantoul, Illinois, opened up his museum for a photo shoot featuring various representatives of the Air Force's Thunderbirds Air Demonstration Team. Once that was done, photographer Kevin Greunwald at Nellis Air Force Base in Nevada also supplied some nice shots of Thunderbird jets in action.

Additional photography came from various other equally willing sources. Bob Peterson, of Cedar Rapids, Iowa, sent along photos of his 1972 T-Bird, which just happens to be the one-millionth 'Bird built. Gene Makrancy, an incredibly energetic enthusiast and automotive historian from Port Vue, Pennsylvania, delivered an image of an experimental Squarebird done in stainless steel. Veteran automotive photographer/writer Tom Glatch FedEx'd his rendition of a 1961 Indy Pace Car 'Bird from Wauwatosa, Wisconsin. Fellow freelancer John Lee did the same with a 1963 "Princess Grace" model. Yet another welcomed photographic addition, this one featuring a pair of T-Birds from 1956 and 1962, came from cohort-in-crime Steve Statham, of Austin, Texas. Just keep rememberin' the Alamo, Steve.

Archival photos came from Dan Erickson at the Ford Photographic Library. Bob Plumer, of Drag Racing Memories (200 N. Kalmia, Highland Springs, Virginia 23075), sent along a Thunderbird Funny Car image, just one of countless historical drag racing photos offered by his company. Other racing shots came from longtime trackside photographers Dorsey Patrick, Phillip Salazar, and Bob Jackson. Donald Farr at Dobbs Publishing Group also saved my bacon with an archival picture or two. Thanks again, Donald–both for the photos and for giving me my start in this business.

Finally, many thanks go to the car owners who shared their pride and joy with my Hasselblad. In general order of appearance, they are: 1957 Thunderbird (blue), Max and Joyce Dilley, Urbana, Illinois; 1955 Thunderbird serial number 0005, George Watts, Orange, California; 1957 Thunderbird (red), Richard and Kathy Goodroe, Annistown, Georgia; 1963 Sports Roadster, Alton Maxwell, Tucker, Georgia; 1960 Thunderbird convertible, Tom Schirra, Marietta, Georgia; 1983 Thunderbird, Harvey and Adella Hodges, Champaign, Illinois; 1964 Thunderbird, Lloyd and Shirley Spellmeyer, Melvin, Illinois; 1979 Thunderbird, Vern Bruner, Rantoul, Illinois; 1956 Thunderbird, Burgess and Angela Stengl, Austin, Texas; 1962 Thunderbird convertible, George and Rosemary Duke, Austin, Texas; 1957 supercharged Thunderbird (white), Kevin and Shellie O'Hara, Orlando, Florida; 1958 Thunderbird convertible, Charlie and Diane Kidd, Palm Coast, Florida; 1963 Thunderbird Landau hardtop, 1963 Sports Roadster, and 1967 Thunderbird four-door, Ken Leaman, Fairfield, New Jersey; 1972 Thunderbird "One-Millionth," Bob Peterson, Cedar Rapids, Iowa; 1975 and 1978 Thunderbirds, Malcolm Green, Califon, New Jersey; 1988 Thunderbird, Vern Bruner, Rantoul, Illinois; 1955 Thunderbird (red), Jim and Carol Lytle, Gotha, Florida; 1997 Thunderbird (last built), Classic Thunderbird Club International, Signal Hill, California; and 1957 Battlebird, Robert "Bo" Cheadle, Pleasanton, California.

The day was September 4, 1997. The place was Ford's Lorain, Ohio, assembly plant. The event was a send-off for the last of a breed. After 43 model runs and 4.3 million cars, Dearborn's high-flying Thunderbird legacy came to a quiet end that evening, almost a full day ahead of schedule. Why pull the plug on one of Detroit's most popular nameplates of all time? Dwindling sales in a market that was being sliced up into smaller and smaller segments had forced Ford's hand. The decision to ground the once-proud T-Bird was nothing personal, it was business, all business. This time there would be no last-minute call from the governor, no listening to nostalgic pleas to preserve a historic legend like those that had saved the Mustang from an unpopular transformation nearly 10 years before.

"Of course we received a ton of calls when we finally made the announcement," said Ford Division Public Affairs Chief Jim Bright. "But once the decision was made, there was no turning back. Ford just let the Thunderbird run its course."

It might have been a sad moment in Lorain last September, yet nary a tear was shed. Dearborn officials did not even mark the moment with any special fanfare for the press. Again, an explanation for their actions was simple: this wasn't good-bye, only farewell for now. As this humble testament goes to press in 1998, Ford Motor Company people are busy working on an all-new Thunderbird, a car scheduled to appear with the coming of the next millennium. Rumors abound concerning plans to bring back the sporty personal-luxury car originally embodied by that classic long-hood, short-deck profile of more than four decades ago.

This is what we know. On May 8, 1998, Ford Automotive Operations President Jac Nasser announced that his company would be reviving the Thunderbird legend not all that far down the road. Nasser's announcement provided just enough information to substantiate rumors.

"A sporty Thunderbird will once again grace America's roads," he said. "Ford owes car lovers everywhere exciting, fun-to-drive vehicles. With the new T-Bird, we

Ford marked the end of a legend in 1997 by donating the very last Thunderbird built to the Classic Thunderbird Club International in Signal Hill, California. Here, the last of the breed poses with what is commonly recognized as the first, CTCI member George Watts' serial number 100005 1955 Thunderbird.

promise to bring back the magic of owning and driving an American icon." Reportedly, this next-generation 'Bird will, in Ford press release words, blend "leading edge technology and world-class driving dynamics and features with design cues true to the heritage of the original T-Bird of the mid-1950s."

According to Nasser, the reborn Thunderbird will be a rear-wheel-drive specialty sports coupe and will share a platform with the Lincoln LS, planned for 2000. Both models will be built at Ford's Wixom assembly plant in Michigan. Recreating the T-Bird ideal is right now in the hands of Chief Program Engineer Nancy Gioia and Chief Designer Doug Gaffka.

So there you have it. All else remains speculation in the summer of 1998. Best guesses put a price in the $30,000 to $35,000 ballpark. And some are predicting that Ford might even install the Mustang Cobra's 4.6-liter V-8, with its overhead cams and 305 horsepower.

All wild guesses about power sources and platform status aside, there is one thing for certain concerning the next all-new Thunderbird—it will be a great car.

This October 1954 ad in the *Saturday Evening Post* jumped the gun a bit. Initial plans to adorn the first Thunderbird with trim similar to the 1955 passenger-line style were scrapped at the last moment.

Three men and their babies—(left to right) retired stylist Alden "Gib" Gilberson, who originally named the Thunderbird; William Boyer, former vice president of design for the 1955 T-Bird; and Jack Telnack, recently retired Ford design chief. The trio met to honor the Thunderbird's 40th anniversary. *Ford Motor Company*

Dearborn's top decision-makers wouldn't have it any other way. They never had any intention of letting such a popular nameplate simply die off, even though they were willing to cut loose all old ties to the existing legend a year ahead of schedule. Squeezing the life out of the T-Bird for one last year before a total rebirth served no purpose except to drag a grand image down. Besides, interrupting the run has only helped heighten anticipation for what's coming next–the greatest Thunderbird yet, perhaps?

Of course, fanatical followers of those first two-seat classics will always make a case against that claim. Dearborn designers in 2000 will undoubtedly remind modern-day buyers of the original Thunderbird ideal, but they will probably never top the "Littlebirds" for the way they captivated the country in 1955, 1956, and 1957. Those epic four-wheel flights of fancy are still able to hypnotize today's car crowd with their stunning style, sex appeal, and timeless impressions. According to a 1992 *USA Today* poll, the 1957 Thunderbird is "America's Favorite Classic Car."

"Named after a legend, it may create one of its own," predicted a January 1955 *Motor Life* report on the newly introduced Thunderbird. Prophecy or understatement? Customers were already showing up in droves at Ford dealers as that article was being written. Orders surpassed 3,500 in just 10 days after the 1955 Thunderbird's public introduction in October 1954. Initial production plans called for

10,000 T-Birds that first year. The final tally was 16,155. After a slight dip in 1956, production of the last–and in most minds the best–two-seat T-Bird in 1957 reached 21,380. Not bad at all for such a narrowly focused automobile, a car that had overnight created its own tight little niche in the American market.

Inspired in rapid-fire fashion by Chevrolet's fiberglass plaything, the Corvette, Ford's first-edition Thunderbird wasn't exactly a sports car–something most observers quickly pointed out. It was too heavy, too luxurious, too comfortable. It had roll-up windows, a big V-8, and power options. Nonetheless, Corvette and Thunderbird were initially classed as rivals, if only because they both had two seats. Hot performance was available in each case, but serious horsepower and handling were the Corvette's realm. Ford in 1955 preferred to label the Thunderbird as a personal driving machine, a tag that soon became "personal luxury." After 1957 these two fun little two-seaters went their separate ways, never to meet again in the same marketing breath.

The Thunderbird ended up taking many different paths itself during its 40-plus years on the road. There remains today some purists who openly insist that Ford stopped building Thunderbirds after 1957. Room for two represented the only way to fly; anything else was blasphemy. Still others consider 1966 the last year. Four doors and accommodations for the entire crew didn't quite cut it for this faction.

But Ford did roll out Thunderbirds each year from 1955 to 1997. In all, 11

True diehards still feel Ford stopped making Thunderbirds after 1957. Still another group gave up the ghost after 1966 when four doors were added into the equation. Shown here are three definitions of pre-1967 personal luxury: a 1957 in front, backed by a 1960 (left), and a 1963 Sports Roadster.

different generations appeared featuring many different cars for many different drivers. Luxury, or at least a modicum of such, has always been included in the deal even if the model in question was no longer so personal. The Thunderbird began small, got bigger, grew huge, shrunk a little, and then got smaller still. The sporty two-seater was replaced by a four-place luxo-cruiser, then a four-door palace on wheels, a trimmed-down show-boat, followed by a downsized market-conscious machine, then an aerodynamic award-winner, and finally a thoroughly modern sports coupe. These changes reflect distinct historical differences in the car's development.

11

In the beginning, the Thunderbird went through a series of "three-year plans." Two-seaters were built from 1955 to 1957, followed by the first four-place 'Birds from 1958 to 1960. Though a disappointment to the fast lane crowd, who preferred their personal luxury in a more intimate, sexier body, the second-generation "Squarebirds" represented the difference between selling like hotcakes and selling by the boatload. Ford Division Chief Robert McNamara's decision to widen the Thunderbird's scope by enlarg-

ing its parameters in 1958 was a wise move, one that kept the 'Bird flying into a new decade. With family men now able to partake in a little Thunderbird prestige, sales of the car almost doubled for 1958 and continued rising each year up through 1960.

Sales slipped a bit, yet remained strong during the "Roundbird's" three-year tenure from 1961 to 1963. Highlighting this period was the super-cool Sports Roadster, a sleek machine that revived still-warm memories of the Thunderbird's

Eleven generations have come and gone since 1955. The 1957 Littlebird in front is joined by the first "Aerobird," introduced in 1983, and a 1964 hardtop.

earliest days thanks to a tonneau cover that hid the back seat beneath twin racing-style headrests. Sports Roadsters were offered in 1962 and 1963.

Buyers could still add the Sports Roadster's tonneau by dealer order in 1964, the year the Thunderbird's fourth three-year installment arrived. In typical fashion, this body style was slightly revamped in 1965. But in 1966, the last of the fourth-generation 'Birds was treated to a few more styling updates in comparison to its Roundbird and Squarebird forerunners in 1963 and 1960, respectively. The final personal luxury T-Bird is easily identified thanks to noticeable trim adjustments at both ends. At a glance, these changes quickly set the 1966 Thunderbird apart from its 1965 and 1964 predecessors. This was also the last year for unitized body/frame construction, which had been a T-Bird trademark since 1958.

A fifth-generation Thunderbird, this one featuring body-on-frame construction, landed in 1967 with a thud. Longer and bigger all over, the 1967 T-Bird was also offered in four-door sedan form—with suicide-style rear doors. There was nothing personal about these luxury monsters. A restyle three years later added six more inches of length, this coming by way of a pronounced "beak" that easily identified the brief sixth-generation T-Bird run of 1970–71.

The seventh-generation Thunderbird grew truly huge in 1972 as Ford's luxury leader basically became a rebadged Lincoln Continental Mk IV. Four-door models were dropped this year, a season

The Thunderbird has certainly been many different cars for many different drivers over its 43-year career. Upsizing, downsizing, it didn't matter—they were all T-Birds. This 1979 'Bird was the last of its generation, a trimmed-down platform first offered in 1977. The Thunderbird was trimmed down even more in 1980.

marked by the production of the one-millionth Thunderbird.

Sportiness (and perhaps sanity) reappeared in 1977 when the slimmer, trimmer, eighth-generation Thunderbird debuted with yet another unitized body, this one shared with the midsized LTD II and Mercury Cougar. Sales skyrocketed to 318,140 that year, then an all-time high for the T-Bird line and a whopping 600 percent increase over the 1976 total. A new record of 352,751 was set in 1978.

And just when it looked like the Thunderbird was soaring like never before, a shift to the three-year-old Fox platform (Ford Fairmont/Mercury Zephyr) in 1980 brought the legacy back down to earth for its ninth-generation run. The downsized, boxy body did little to enhance the T-Bird image, nor did weak-kneed engineering. As if Ford's small-block V-8s of that era weren't bad enough, a six-cylinder was also introduced into the T-Bird mix for the first time. Status and prestige ebbed away during this weakly received three-year run.

A totally fresh image debuted in 1983. Sleek and rakish, the 10th-generation T-Bird was based on a revamped Fox-chassis platform. On top, this "Aero Luxury Car" cut through the wind to the tune of a 0.35 drag coefficient, not bad for a car that just one year before had featured all the aerodynamics of a brick. Performance was also enhanced by the midyear appearance of the popular Turbo Coupe with its forced-induction 2.3-liter four-cylinder engine. Buyers couldn't resist, and Thunderbird sales in 1983 jumped 170 percent compared to 1982's feeble results. "Aerobird" popularity remained strong throughout this generation's six-year life span.

An even more aerodynamic body draped over a new MN12 chassis featuring independent rear suspension drew

Forty years after one of the greatest American classics hit the streets, Ford rolled out its last Thunderbird for 1997. These bookend 'Birds are joined by a few of the high-flying machines of Kermit Weeks' Fantasy of Flight Aviation Museum in Polk City, Florida.

The Thunderbird's public farewell came in November 1997 at NASCAR's NAPA 500 in Atlanta. Here Mark Martin pilots his T-Bird for the last time. In 1998, he and the other Ford drivers traded their 'Birds for Taurus four-doors.

major raves in 1989 as the final member of the Thunderbird family bowed. And in place of the Turbo Coupe, which had disappeared along with the last Fox-chassis 'Bird in 1988, came the exciting Super Coupe powered by a 210-horsepower supercharged 3.8-liter V-6. Blown SC Thunderbirds were offered up only through 1995 while the MN12 platform rolled on in painfully similar form through nine model years. What made such grand headlines in 1989 became old news in a hurry as customers in the 1990s watched as basically the same old Thunderbird came and went year in, year out. The repetitive nature of the last-generation Thunderbird, however, shouldn't obscure the plain truth that all the MN12 'Birds were fine automobiles. To the end, they lived up to the Thunderbird name with pride.

Proof of just how well respected the 11th-generation T-Bird was came in 1989 courtesy of *Motor Trend* magazine, which honored the 1989 T-Bird SC as "Car of the Year." Two other Thunderbirds had previously driven home with "Car of the Year" trophies: the first Squarebird in 1958 and the upgraded 1987 Turbo Coupe. Another high-profile honor had come in 1961 when a Thunderbird convertible was chosen as the prestigious pace car for the Indianapolis 500.

Ford image-makers created special moments more than once to hype important dates in Thunderbird history. For example, all T-Birds in 1975 were considered 20th Anniversary models. Specially painted and trimmed models also appeared in 1980 and 1990 to mark the 'Bird's 25th and 35th birthdays, respectively. Dearborn didn't officially honor the 40th Thunderbird in 1995, but dealers were more than willing to stripe one up for you in full commemorative fashion. Whether or not Ford will let the car's 50th anniversary go by uncelebrated in 2005 is anyone's guess. Of course, they'll need to have another next-generation Thunderbird up and running first.

And you can bet when that happens horns will blow and confetti will fly.

Chapter 1

T-Bird for Two
1955-1957

Forty-three model runs—that's how many different T-Birds there have been. Few other long-running automotive nameplates have known longevity like that. Right now, only Chevrolet's Corvette can claim a longer production life.

Yet, despite those 43 successful years and 4.3 million cars sold up through 1997, many bystanders, innocent or otherwise, still only pay homage to Ford's first three Thunderbirds, the beloved two-seaters that sped off with so many hearts nearly a half century ago. "Littlebirds," "Earlybirds," or whatever you want to call them, the original Thunderbirds were, are, and always will remain the only T-Birds worth remembering as far as many fanatic followers are concerned. Indeed, in these minds, Ford stopped making Thunderbirds after 1957. Squarebirds,

Resemblances between the first two-seat Thunderbirds and the full-sized Ford line were made additionally apparent thanks to this trim treatment, which just missed regular production. Like Ford's standard passenger cars, the 1955 Thunderbird also would've probably been offered with two-tone paint. *Ford Motor Company*

Although a 1955 Thunderbird wearing serial number 100004 is now believed to exist, this black beauty, owned by longtime T-Bird enthusiast George Watts, is still recognized as the "first" Thunderbird. Its serial number is 100005. It has long been assumed that any cars built before Watts' were used for testing, not for public sale.

Roundbirds, Bigbirds, Aerobirds; it doesn't matter. The rest are impostors. All of them.

OK, so maybe there have been way too many fences built way too tall among the Thunderbird faithful over the years. Biases are still strong, even after 43 years. Why can't we all just get along? Perhaps because we really don't have to, at least not as far as honoring famous automobiles of the past is concerned. Thunderbirds have meant so many different things to so many different people during their historic run, that to group them under one banner would be unjust to all sides. Each individual faction deserves its own distinctive niche in automotive history. Yet, despite complaints that they're allowed to unfairly overshadow their successors, those first three T-Birds do receive the lion's share of nostalgic kudos, perhaps more so than all the following models combined.

Few automobiles, domestic or foreign, have ever inspired as much awe as the

Misguided assumptions that Ford's first Thunderbirds were sports cars weren't hindered in the least by the presence of a standard tachometer, located at the instrument panel's far left corner.

original Thunderbird. And even fewer have shown such long legs. More than four decades after the last of the two-seat breed became history, the first-generation T-Bird easily ranks right up at the top with any of the most recognized, respected, and revered cars to ever roll out of Detroit.

Even people who couldn't care less about cars will stop and smile when a two-seat 'Bird rolls by. That long-hood/short-deck profile, the portholes added in 1956, and those little fins that sprouted in 1957.

You can't swing a dead cat by the tail and not hit someone able to identify these features at a glance. Not being able to do so would be un-American. Forget baseball, apple pie, and Chevrolet—red, white, and blue icons don't come much more patriotic than the two-seat Thunderbird. When Dearborn's movers and shakers first began building Thunderbirds, they may well have captured the very essence of what makes a great American car.

Great American car buyers in 1954 had never seen anything quite like it. More than one witness mentioned that the long-hood, short-deck look harkened back to Edsel Ford's classic Lincoln Continentals of 1940—interestingly, similar comparisons would be made in 1964 between the original T-Bird and Lee Iacocca's all-new Mustang. More specifically, an obvious connection could've been made between the first Thunderbird and its natural rival, Chevrolet's Corvette.

Some say the first T-Bird was a Corvette knock-off. Trying to find a truly original idea in Detroit has never been an easy task and remains especially tough today. Ford in the 1950s was no exception, nor was Chevrolet.

The whole two-seat phenomenon came into being thanks to a little overseas inspiration. American servicemen coming home from the war in Europe brought back more than medals. Some were transformed by their first experience seeing and driving a British sports car.

The affliction spread slowly at first. As the 1950s dawned, American drivers began to feel a new itch, an achin' for makin'

Thunderbird serial numbers began in the 100,000 range. And for years, this plate, the fifth issued, was the lowest known entry in that progression for 1955.

Most drivers in this country were still turned off by the European roadster's inherently rude, crude nature. Sewing machine motors, leaky tops, pesky side curtains, uncomfortably close quarters, and few conveniences were all drawbacks in the American car market. And stingy sales figures showed that America really didn't want a sports car in the 1950s—a European-style sports car, that is.

Early Corvettes were rolling proof of just what the U.S. market *would* accept in those days. Chevrolet's intriguing two-seater nearly died after only two years on the road, due to its all-too-close resemblance to the bare-bones British sporting breed and its lackluster drivetrain, which consisted of a yeoman six-cylinder backed by a Powerglide automatic transmission. The Corvette didn't find real success until Chevy designers wised up and repackaged their fiberglass flight of fancy in a more user-friendly fashion. Also thrown in were more power, more performance, and more practicality. Life-saving additions included a V-8 in 1955 and a three-speed manual transmission very late that year. Exterior door handles, roll-up windows, and an optional removable hardtop joined the mix in 1956. Presto, "America's sports car" was born and Corvette drivers haven't looked back since.

Ford officials, along with legions of showgoers, had their first look at the original Corvette in January 1953 during the GM Motorama in New York. Who cared that the market for such a playboy's toy then accounted for about 1/4 of 1 percent of total car sales in this country? What

tracks, a need for speed, or at least the sensation of such. Top-down travel in a tight roadster that handled the curves with unprecedented confidence became the release, a new freedom. Imagining that a car could be fun and frivolous, and that going from point A to point B didn't have to be a chore, meant it could really be an adventure. But while the classic European sports car ideal *was* finding a home in this country during the early 1950s, not all that many Yankees were convinced it could survive here long.

Unlike Corvettes, which initially came only with six-cylinder power, the Thunderbird was a V-8 cruiser from the get-go. Ford's Y-block V-8, introduced in 1954, fell right in place beneath the 1955 T-Bird's scooped hood. Displacement was 292 cubic inches.

mattered was the fact that Chevrolet had beaten Ford to the sports car punch. Even though the fledgling sports car field represented shaky economic ground, Dearborn decision-makers weren't about to idly stand by while the Corvette rolled out unchallenged.

One month after the Motorama show, word was sent down from the top at Ford to develop a comparable two-seater pronto. Ford General Manager Lewis Crusoe's team wasted even less time than Chevy's crew had while rushing the Corvette to market. Chief Engineer William Burnett oversaw the car's

mechanicals, while William Boyer, under the direction of legendary designer Frank Hershey, did the bulk of the styling work. Together, they had a completed form all but finalized by February 1954. The big debut came at the Detroit Auto Show with a wooden mock-up that soon had both the press and the public clamoring for the real thing.

Motor Trend's Don MacDonald was among the first to herald the arrival of something truly new on the Detroit scene. He wrote that Ford appeared ready to not only meet Chevrolet's challenge, but to do it one better. Like

Contrasting this 1956 'Bird is a 1962 convertible. In 1956, output for the standard 292 V-8 was increased to 202 horsepower. *Steve Statham*

MacDonald, nearly all who saw the Thunderbird mock-up in Detroit recognized that the only aspect copied from the Corvette was the topless body with two-passenger seating and a short, 102-inch wheelbase. From the very beginning, Crusoe's plan had involved creating not a direct sports car competitor for the Corvette but an unquestionably fresh combination of youthful, sporty flair and outstanding prestige, all tied up in a package that was reasonably practical and wonderfully frivolous at the same time.

MacDonald's one-page April 1954 *MT* report, entitled "Thunderin' Thunderbird," explained that Crusoe had insisted that his designers stick with a metal body, not fiberglass, in order to keep manufacturing difficulties down while speeding production up. Clearly, Ford intended to build T-Birds faster, and in greater numbers than Chevrolet could mold up its Corvette.

The idea was not only to produce more cars, but to produce more car. "Perhaps the outstanding feature of the new Ford Thunderbird is the clever wedding of sports car functionalism with American standards of comfort," wrote MacDonald. Unlike the Corvette, the very first Thunderbird would have roll-up windows, a removable hardtop, and standard V-8 power. Chevrolet customers in search of fun behind the wheel of an automobile were still awaiting these warmly welcomed features.

Another Ford priority involved how quickly and easily the Thunderbird could be designed and built. Like the Corvette, which had many off-the-shelf passenger-car parts hidden beneath that innovative fiberglass shell, the first 'Bird relied on as

Noticeably new features for the 1956 Thunderbird included windwings for the windshield frame, cowl vents in the fenders, and the soon-to-be-popular "portholes" for the removable hardtop. Hardtops in 1956 came with or without portholes. They were essentially offered as a no-cost option.

A cleaner, revised grille/bumper layout announced the arrival of the third two-seat Thunderbird in 1957.

many "family ties" as possible to reach regular production. But, unlike the Chevy, Ford's two-seater also showed its passenger-line heritage on the outside. The fact that the original Thunderbird looked very much like a scaled-down 1955 Ford was no coincidence. Reportedly, the car's rapid-fire design process began with Bill Burnett's engineers simply cutting a standard 1955 sedan apart and welding it back together on that shortened 102-inch wheelbase.

From there, many styling cues followed closely along the lines of Ford's new full-sized look for 1955. From its hooded headlights to its round taillights, the Thunderbird was clearly every inch a Ford.

The easiest way to identify a 1956 Thunderbird is by its standard Continental kit spare tire carrier, which many felt didn't do the car any favors from a ride and handling perspective. The spare would go back inside an enlarged trunk in 1957.

Probably the most widely recognized classic T-Bird trademark is its "porthole" opera windows, first introduced as an option for the 'Bird's removable hardtop in 1956. They were so popular many believed they came standard. This is a 1957 hardtop.

Designers even considered using bodyside trim identical to the full-sized line—the so-called "Fairlane stripe." The thought was that two-tone paint options, similar to those used by the big Fairlanes, would then fit the little 'Birds to a "T" as well. At least one, and perhaps two prototypes were finished with the Fairlane trim, and an early advertisement in late 1954 even depicted the finalized Thunderbird

form with this trim. Fortunately the idea was discarded at the last moment—the first 'Bird looked much better with less rather than more.

Early plans also hinted at using the Fairlane name—also the moniker of Henry Ford's estate—for the new two-seater. Instead, a corporation-wide contest was held offering $250 to the employee who could best name the breed. Stylist Alden "Gib" Gilberson took the prize, which ended up being a suit in place of the cash. A native of the American Southwest, Gilberson turned to familiar Native American mythology for his inspiration. Thunderbird was a legendary name for a soon-to-be-legendary car.

Production of Ford's legend began on September 9, 1954, with the Thunderbird officially going on sale to the public October 22. Teased for most of the previous year, customers couldn't get into dealerships fast enough to buy a car that left many wondering exactly what they were seeing. It looked like a sports car. It was small and light and fast, yet it impressed like a luxury car. It was also comfortable and had a much smoother ride than Chevy's Corvette.

Reporters weren't even sure what Ford had wrought. "The accusation that American car manufacturers couldn't build a sports car—even if they tried—is no longer valid," wrote Walt Woron of *Motor Trend*. "The first indication was the Chevrolet Corvette. And although the Ford Motor Co. is the first one to deny it, they have a sports car in the Thunderbird, and it's a good one."

Road & Track's editors, who preferred covering true sports cars over anything else, were not so quick to call a spade a spade. "The first truly American 'personal' car is the way the Ford Motor Company describes their new 2/3 seater, high-performance Thunderbird," began an October 1954 *R&T* report. "To the purist the Thunderbird has far too much luxury to qualify as a sports car, but even that group will find much of interest in the specifications of this car."

Most interesting was the power source, a bored-out version of Ford's 272-cid Y-block V-8. Featuring a single four-barrel carburetor, 8.1:1 compression, and dual exhausts, the standard 292-cid Thunderbird V-8 injected 193 healthy horses into the two-seat equation—when the base three-speed manual transmission was chosen. Adding the optional Ford-O-Matic automatic transmission also brought along a slight compression increase to 8.5:1, meaning output in turn

More optional underhood thunder was added in 1956 as the Y-block was enlarged to 312 cubic inches. With a single four-barrel carburetor shooting the juice in 1957, the 312 Thunderbird V-8 produced 245 horsepower.

A lengthened trunk allowed designers to hide the spare tire back beneath the rear decklid in 1957. Crowning the 1957 'Bird's new tail was a pair of humble fins atop each taillight. Powering this example is the rare supercharged 312 V-8.

went up 5 horses to 198. Performance was commonly listed as 0-60 in about nine seconds. The top end was right about 120 miles per hour.

Standard 1955 Thunderbird equipment also included a removable fiberglass hardtop, at least it did after some early confusion was cleared up. Apparently some early cars came standard with no top at all, since both the lift-off hardtop and folding soft top were initially listed in factory paperwork as options along with

conveniences like power windows and a power seat. Eventually, however, the hardtop was included in the base price of about $3,000. Adding a convertible top in place of the hardtop cost an additional $75. Price for both tops was $290.

With the top off or down, a T-Bird driver received a decent dose of sports car feel, an impression backed up by all the horsepower supplied beneath that polite little hood scoop. With the hardtop on, passengers were comforted in the knowledge that they didn't have to arrive at the club with the Don King look. Your hair not only stayed in place, it also remained dry. Such sporty performance had never come so classy and convenient before. Maybe that's why the first Thunderbird outsold Chevrolet's 1955 Corvette by a 23-to-1 margin.

Plans to sell 20,000 T-Birds in 1956 proved a bit optimistic. Nonetheless, 15,631 'Birds out the door the second time around was certainly nothing to sneeze at, and that for a car only slightly updated. Noticeably new features for the 1956 Thunderbird included windwings for the windshield frame, cowl vents in the fenders, and the soon-to-be-popular "portholes" for the removable hardtop. Hardtops in 1956 came with or without portholes as they were essentially offered as a no-cost option.

To make room in the trunk, designers also moved the spare tire outside into a classic-style Continental carrier mounted on the rear bumper. Other more subtle changes in back included moving the dual exhaust exits to the bumper's corners (since the Continental kit now blocked the position used in 1955) and slightly revising the taillights.

A floor shifter and engine-turned dash face enhanced the Thunderbird's sporty image from behind the wheel. The small circular device suspended from the dashboard below the radio is the memory control for the optional Dial-A-Matic power seat. A driver could set this control for height (five choices) or front-to-back preferences (seven choices). When the key was turned off, the seat moved rearward to allow easy exit and re-entry. Once the key was turned back on, the seat would then return back to its preset position. This option was offered only in 1957.

Ford briefly turned up the heat for the Thunderbird early in 1957, offering two race-ready engine options. The first choice added twin four-barrel carburetors atop the 312 Y-block pushing output to 270 horses.

Underhood upgrades for 1956 were both subtle and serious. First, output for the 292 V-8 was increased to 202 horsepower. The really big news, however, was the introduction of the enlarged 312-cid Y-block, which was available with either 215 or 225 horses. Chevy's Corvette that year was also advertised with 225 horsepower. By the end of 1956, there were nearly four times as many Thunderbirds on the road as Corvettes. Consider also that Chevy had a two-year head start on production.

In 1957, the third-edition Thunderbird's spare tire was put back inside the car as the trunk was lengthened some six inches. Helping announce this restyle were outward-canted fins atop each rear quarter. These were courtesy of Frank Hershey, who had played a major role in GM's introduction of the fin fad while

working at Cadillac in 1948. Up front, a new and larger grille and a revised bumper came along with the last of the two-seat T-Birds. Throw in a few other minor updates and you have what most consider to be the best of the breed. Buyers apparently agreed. Ford did finally break the 20,000-unit sales barrier in 1957.

Adding to the 1957 Thunderbird's attraction was even more strength beneath that long, long hood. Output for the 292 and 312 Y-blocks that year increased to 212 and 245 horsepower, respectively. And that wasn't all.

From the beginning, Thunderbirds' V-8s had used single carburetors to handle fuel metering chores. Then, late in 1956, Ford tried a dual–four-barrel intake for the 312 Y-block, this addition reportedly boosting horsepower to 265. In

1957, the twin Holley carb option was offered again as part of the "E-code" Thunderbird Special V-8 package, rated at 270 horses. Adding the "NASCAR kit" cam upped the E-Bird's output to 285 horsepower. But if that didn't light your fire, there was more.

The hottest Thunderbird V-8 in 1957 used only one Holley four-barrel. Attached to that carburetor, however, was a McCulloch centrifugal supercharger supplying as much as six pounds of boost by way of its belt-driven impeller. Advertised output for the "F-code" supercharged 312 was 300 horsepower; 340 with the solid-lifter NASCAR cam. Only 208 F-Birds were built, 14 of those being the "D/F" versions built specially in January 1957 with NASCAR tracks in mind. Estimates put twin-carb E-Bird production at about 500.

Both models E and F came and went quickly during the first half of the 1957 model year as Ford was forced to change its plan for taking its high-flying Y-blocks racing. In June 1957, the Automobile Manufacturers Association issued what amounted to be a ban on such "unsafe" shenanigans. Initially offered for both the Thunderbird and Ford's passenger-car line, the dual-carb and supercharged 312 V-8s were immediately canceled right about the time of the AMA decree, victims of a newfound need in Detroit to curb what some considered to be a horsepower race running out of bounds.

Ford's two-seat T-Bird followed those high-powered engines into history a few months later, much to the dismay of so many Thunderbird lovers who never were able to warm up to the four-place 'Birds that followed.

Top power in 1957 came from this supercharged 312, which used a belt-driven blower to boost output to 300 horses. Adding an optional solid-lifter cam reportedly unleashed another 40 horsepower.

Chapter 2

Four is More
1958-1966

Time sometimes has a strange way of wounding all heals. Consider the fate of the Squarebird, a car totally undeserving of the slings and arrows hurled its way by modern-day second-guessers. Sure, a great number of the people who had fallen madly for the two-seat Thunderbird were wholly disappointed when room for two more was added in 1958. Yet, those complaints aside, the first four-place T-Bird still emerged as an unqualified success, perhaps even an overnight sensation.

A refocused target market thought so. After a late introduction, the 1958 Thunderbird managed to establish a new sales standard for the breed—and this in a recession-wracked year of disaster when no one in Detroit was selling cars. No one but Ford, that is. The redesigned four-seat 'Bird was one of only two American models in 1958 to lay claim to a sales increase, in this case a whopping 76 percent jump

It may have broken purists' hearts, but the first "Squarebird" saved the bloodline from extinction in 1958. The totally redesigned 1958 Thunderbird used unit-body construction in place of the body-on-frame platform found beneath the two-seat 'Bird.

Designers saved the Thunderbird from an early grave by widening its appeal in 1958. Key to this new direction was adding seating for two more passengers. A nonstock radio has been added by this 1958 T-Bird's owner.

over 1957's results. Depressed economy be damned, Dearborn successfully rolled out 37,892 Thunderbirds in 1958. Another 67,456 followed in 1959, then 92,843 in 1960–the latter a record high that would stand until 1977. Clearly something was right about the car.

Most of the motor press in 1958 supported this claim to a great degree.

According to *Motor Life*, the 1958 T-Bird was "probably the most modern American car in production." In the words of *Motor Trend*'s editors, it was "a car that combines safety with performance and comfort with compactness." The *MT* staff was so impressed, they picked the first Squarebird as their "Car of the Year" for 1958. A second "Car of the Year" trophy wouldn't come Thunderbird's way for another 30 years.

All that pomp and circumstance, all that sales success, yet the four-place Thunderbird still commonly gets a bum revisionist rap. Purists never have forgotten or forgiven. Inspired by their often loud cries of "foul," a car-loving public concerned more with nostalgic memories than historic fact has bought into the belief that Dearborn's decision to repackage the T-Bird in 1958 was a mistake. Stop any motorist with fuzzy dice hanging from the rearview mirror of his car today and ask him what he thinks. Chances are he will regurgitate a familiar line, "Ford stopped building Thunderbirds in 1957."

In truth, Dearborn probably would have done just that had Robert McNamara not come to the rescue with a bigger,

A three-year production run remained a Thunderbird practice into the Squarebird years. After 1960, the first of the four-place T-Bird bodystyles was replaced by the radically updated "Roundbird," which in turn rolled on through three more years. This convertible Squarebird is one of 11,860 built for 1960.

Standard Squarebird power came from Ford's new 352-cid FE-series V-8. As it had in 1958, this 352 Interceptor V-8 was still producing 300 horsepower for the 1960 Thunderbird.

better idea for 1958. Later criticized for his conservative ways, Ford's sales-conscious division chief was the main man behind the Thunderbird's radical redesign. "He fought with the board of directors to get it, and he won the fight," wrote designer Bill Boyer later in reference to the four-place 'Bird proposal.

McNamara did have eyes. He could see the limited appeal of the two-seat Thunderbird, and he could also read a balance sheet, where the ink wasn't anywhere near as black as Ford officials had hoped, despite three years of increasing sales. Many Ford officials were already doubting the T-Bird's ability to sustain extended flight as early as December 1954. Once McNamara rose to the general manager's seat not long afterward, he almost immediately took up the cause of keeping the Thunderbird alive at all costs. It was clear to him that a 'Bird of another feather would be required to carry on the breed, and soon.

Widening the car's appeal was the obvious answer, and increasing seating was the

36

key to widening that appeal. Two may have been cool, but four was more. More room for more people to fit inside. More reasons for more people to rush into Ford dealerships. More sales. More Thunderbirds.

Most at Ford recognized a bigger 'Bird was not that far down the road even as the first Littlebird was turning heads everywhere in 1955. Product planner Tom Case even proposed a two-model lineup where the two-seater would continue in production, joined by a four-seat running mate. McNamara, however, shot this idea down. It would be four-place or no place for the future T-Bird. A full roof would also enclose the car for the first time as part of the plan to bring the Thunderbird closer to the mainstream.

But what about the Thunderbird's sports car image? Or its "personal luxury" place in Ford Motor Company's pecking order? Wouldn't more seats, more room, and more size negate these impressions? *Road & Track* came forth with an immediate answer to these questions in its February 1958 issue:

"While sports car fiends generally have not been too kind to the Thunderbird (an understatement), they should remember three things: (1) The Ford Motor Company has never called the T-Bird a sports car; it is a personal car, if you

In July 1960, Ford, working in concert with the Budd Body Company and Allegheny-Ludlum Steel, produced two experimental Thunderbirds on the Wixom assembly line using complete stainless-steel structures. They were the last two Squarebirds built, as officials knew the "less cooperative" stainless steel would ruin the body stamping dies. This stainless 1960 T-Bird still survives at Allegheny-Ludlum's Pennsylvania works. *Gene Makrancy*

The first Roundbird was chosen as the prestigious pace car for the 1961 Indianapolis 500, its golden finish helping mark the 50th anniversary of the fabled Brickyard's first Memorial Day race. *Tom Glatch*

please. (2) Most Americans like luxury and will never accept the starkness of a true sports car. (3) Many T-Bird owners are willing and frequent converts to the fun-driving features of genuine dual-purpose sports cars."

There it was. The Thunderbird never really was a sports car, it was a sporty luxury car. More to the point, it was a sporty personal luxury car. And since Ford people basically defined "personal luxury," they could build it in any fashion they wanted. "As a result of their own surveys," explained *Road & Track*'s report, "Ford decided that their personal car should be a four-seater."

Ford basically considered the four-place Thunderbird hardtop to be a refinement of the personal luxury idea, even though the car was considerably less personal than its two-seat forerunner thanks to its bigger body. Most early responses to the 1958 T-Bird included references to the car's clear family ties to Lincoln's truly huge Continentals, a connection that ran deeper than casual witnesses realized since both models relied on Ford's new unitized body/frame construction, and thus shared the same production line at the equally new assembly plant in Wixom, Michigan.

On the one hand, exterior impressions of the 1958 T-Bird were quite "Lincolnesque." They clearly represented a distinct departure from the breed's sporty beginnings. As *Motor Life*'s reviewers explained it, "the ['58] Thunderbird boasts a new maturity which past enthusiasts may call conservative."

Looks, on the other hand, were deceiving. Despite the fact that the 1958 T-Bird appeared to dwarf its predecessors, it still retained some of that warm and fuzzy feeling first offered in 1955. Compared to Detroit's incredibly huge, overstuffed luxury showboats of the late 1950s, the 1958 Thunderbird was very much a "personal car." Its four-place bucket seat interior with console was completely comfortable and warmly welcoming to drivers looking for a little pizzazz and prestige in a relatively polite package. It was also seriously cool, with a sporty feel behind the wheel that remained a T-Bird trademark, even though the car now wore a full time steel roof and looked more like a luxury liner on the outside.

Making room for two more riders required a stretched 113-inch wheelbase for the Squarebird's unitized platform—11 inches longer than the Littlebird's chassis. Overall length went up two feet, width increased by six inches and weight jumped up about a half a ton. An exceptionally low 5.8-inch ground clearance kept roof height down, something designers planned all along. Trends of the day dictated longer, lower, wider lines for the 1958 Thunderbird, which in turn accentuated the car's newfound mass.

Two new variations on the Thunderbird theme were introduced in 1962: the prestigious Landau hardtop and sexy Sports Roadster. This black Landau is one of 12,139 built for 1963.

Along with a vinyl roof and classic landau bars, the Thunderbird Landau also featured various interior dress-ups. Simulated walnut trim was part of the deal.

Also new for the 1958 platform were coil springs in back. These were added in the hopes of incorporating the division's "Ford Aire" air suspension. However, once those air springs fizzled beneath Ford's standard line in the fall of 1958, they were nixed from the Thunderbird layout as well.

Dealer introductions of the four-place Thunderbird began on February 13, 1958, more than four months after other "new-for-'58" Fords. A total redesign typically took longer than planned. Official production at

Wixom had begun on January 13 and initially only included hardtop models. With approval for a topless Squarebird not coming until May 1957, convertible production was also delayed. The first 1958 T-Bird convertible—with semiautomatic power top operation—didn't appear on showroom floors until June 1958.

Power for the Squarebird came from Ford's new FE-series V-8. Displacement was 352 cubic inches; output was 300 horsepower. Engineers reportedly considered offering the 361-cid Edsel V-8 as an

In February 1963, Ford introduced a special limited-edition Landau model in Monaco, where Princess Grace was given the first such example. Only 2,000 were built, all painted white with white leather interiors and deep maroon vinyl tops. *John Lee*

Stunning Kelsey-Hayes wire wheels were included as part of the Sports Roadster package along with that distinctive tonneau cover that converted the car back into a classic two-seater. Only 455 Sports Roadsters were built for 1963, including this red-hot example.

option, and some claim the 375 horsepower 430-cid Lincoln V-8 did make the Thunderbird list late in the year. While the former never got beyond the planning stage, the latter did at least appear in prototype form for a *Motor Trend* road test in 1958. However, actual production of 430-powered 'Birds that year is doubted.

The big 430 V-8, in this case rated at 350 horsepower, did become an official Thunderbird option in 1959, when a second Squarebird appeared in nearly identical fashion, save for a new grille and different trim for the bodysides and taillights. After spending $5 million rebuilding the T-Bird for 1958, Ford was only able to set aside another $2 million to update the second-generation Thunderbird through its planned three-year run. Unfortunately, design work on the "afterthought" 1958 convertible had taken a major bite out of that future budget, thus the reason for so few upgrades.

More minor trim adjustments and a switch from four taillights to six announced the 1960 Thunderbird's arrival. Other improvements during the Squarebird's run included the addition of a fully automatic convertible top late in 1959 and the introduction of this country's first postwar sunroof, a manually controlled hardtop option offered in 1960. Additionally, the coil spring suspension used in 1958 was traded for traditional leaf springs for 1959 and 1960.

Three-year generations continued to be a Thunderbird tradition through the four-place run. The last Squarebird was

Thunderbird interiors never lacked appeal, and the 1963 Sports Roadster was no exception. Notice the console-mounted tachometer.

One of the hottest Thunderbird engine options of all time was the M-code 390-cid V-8 fed by three Holley two-barrel carburetors. Introduced in 1962, this triple-carb FE-series big-block put out 340 horsepower. This M-code application is beneath a 1963 Sports Roadster's hood. Only 37 340-horse Sports Roadsters were built that year.

hustled out the door early in July 1960 to make room for the restyled, aeronautically inspired Roundbird, which rolled on, once more, in nearly identical fashion up through 1963. The last three-year group of the four-place family featured even more modern, truly crisp styling, which in turn led to a new rise in popularity. The 1964 Thunderbird outsold its 1963 predecessor by almost 30,000 units, nearly setting a new sales standard in the process. Final production that year was 92,465. At 69,176, Thunderbird sales were still healthy two years later for the four-place 'Bird's final flight, but 1966 was also the last time a convertible T-Bird was offered.

Technical highlights from the third- and fourth-generation runs included a typical displacement escalation, first to 390 cubic inches in 1961, then to 428 cubes for another FE-series big-block V-8 introduced as an option in 1966. An optional "Swing-Away" steering wheel was introduced in 1961, an intriguing feature that enhanced a wonderfully sporty interior that was all but unmatched in Detroit for its sexy style. Front disc brakes and sequential taillights also became standard equipment in 1965.

Milestones included an appearance at "The Brickyard" in 1961 as the prestigious pace car for the Indianapolis 500. Two new models were unveiled in 1962, one created to enhance the Thunderbird's luxury reputation, the other intended to revive memories of the car's two-seat heritage.

The first, a Landau hardtop, added a standard vinyl roof with classically inspired "landau irons" on each rear pillar. Simulated walnut interior appointments became part of the standard Landau hardtop deal in 1963. A special-edition "Princess Grace" (or "Monaco") Landau was also introduced in February 1963. All 2,000 built featured white paint, Rose Beige vinyl roofs, white leather upholstery, and simulated rosewood interior accents. A special serial number plate on the dash was the crowning touch. A second limited-edition Landau hardtop model appeared in March 1965, this one featuring Emberglo paint with matching wheelcovers and interior appointments. A dash-mounted serial number plate again marked these cars, of which 4,500 were built.

The second Thunderbird variation that debuted in 1962 came in response to all those complaints first heard in 1958. Amazingly, two-seat purists' protests didn't all fall on deaf ears. As early as 1960, work had begun on a new type of sporty T-Bird, thanks to Ford Marketing Manager Lee Iacocca, who apparently felt that those who helped make the first Thunderbirds a soaring success shouldn't be left flat. More to the truth, Iacocca was bombarded with requests from dealers for a return to the two-seat theme. The result was the Sports Roadster, the sexy topless T-Bird with that tight-fitting tonneau that converted a four-place Roundbird into a two-seat tourer.

The idea wasn't exactly new. As early as 1958, New Jersey Ford dealer Bill Booth had been manufacturing fiberglass rear seat tonneau covers for Squarebird convertibles. With the groundwork established, it didn't take long for Ford designers to try the same trick on their own. Credited primarily to stylist Bud Kaufman, the Sports Roadsters' fiberglass tonneau fit almost like a glove and at the same time allowed the convertible top to operate unheeded. Twin headrests, which were more stylish than functional, were incorporated into the cover. The package

While the Sports Roadster model was dropped after 1963, Thunderbird buyers could still dealer-order a similar tonneau cover in 1964. *Ford Motor Company*

also featured exclusive fender emblems, a dash-mounted grab bar, and four dazzling Kelsey-Hayes wire wheels.

Sports Roadsters were offered in both 1962 and 1963, each wearing heavy price tags: $5,439 in 1962, and $5,563 in 1963. Those numbers help explain why buyers stayed away in droves. Production was only 1,427 in 1962, a mere 455 the following year.

Even more rare were the "M-code" Sports Roadsters. In January 1962, Ford officially introduced the M-code engine option, a $242 package that exchanged the standard Z-code 390 V-8's four-barrel carburetor for three Holley two-barrels. Output for the "390-6V" big-block was 340 horsepower, increased by 40 horses from the Z engine. And along with various engineering tweaks, the M-code Thunderbird V-8 also wore a nice dose of chrome-plated dress-up pieces.

M-code T-Bird production was meager to say the least–145 in 1962, 55 in 1963. Sports Roadsters made up the bulk of these installations (the option was available for four-place 'Birds, too), totaling 120 in 1962, and 37 in 1963. Even though the six-barrel Sports Roadster probably ranks as the sportiest Thunderbird ever, its limited-edition presence allowed it to escape the attentions of most casual observers. Too bad–this was the one member of the family that truly did put the thunder in Thunderbird.

Ford's final four-place Thunderbird body debuted in 1964 to the apparent delight of customers who couldn't get enough. Sales soared from 63,313 for the last Roundbird to 92,465 for the restyled 1964 'Bird.

T-Birds in Pop Culture

Bestowing larger-than-life status on favored subjects is a practice Americans can't resist. Call it a need to look up to something, or classify it as an addiction to nostalgia. Whatever the reason, we tend to hand out immortality I.D. cards to people and things as if we have the power to restore life to the former, or create it for the latter. In both cases, that artificial life called fame almost always grows in prominence as time marches on.

Marilyn Monroe wasn't just an actress (some feel she wasn't even an actress), she was the personification of sex—soft, slow, slithering, steamy sex. In life, Norma Jean Baker was the "It Girl" for the 1950s generation. In death, she has become so highly revered by the baby boomer crowd, men and women alike, that her image has been purified almost to the point of restoring her virginity. No one today dares imagine her photographic phantom in unclad fashion, something *Playboy* readers had actually witnessed in 1953.

As in Marilyn's case, the jury is also still out on Elvis Presley. Sure his songs were fun, his attraction was electric, but his lyrical contributions to musical history were far from classic. His celluloid efforts were even less so. Yet his ghost continues to stalk us at convenience stores all across the country. Elvis had already reached a larger-than-life place (in more ways than one) during his last few years. After his alleged death, he really began throwing his weight around. To most fans today Elvis wasn't just a rock star, he was (and still is) The King. "Larger" isn't a big enough word.

Then there's the classic Thunderbird. Nostalgic icons may not come much larger, certainly not in the automotive realm. This wasn't just a car, it was an E-ticket ride to the fountain of youth. A two-seat T-Bird worked better than a toupee as a youthful tonic in 1955. Nearly a half century later the car still revives fond remembrances of yesterday. Even fans of the fabled '57 Chevy have to admit that their fave takes a backseat to the "Earlybird" in the race down memory lane. Pick up a "Lost in the '50s" T-shirt today and chances are it will immortalize one of at least three major icons — Norma Jean, The King, or a '57 T-Bird.

Ford's first Thunderbirds probably didn't need much help becoming hallowed pieces of Americana automotive art. Their

Elvira, B-movie queen, is the proud owner of a ghoulishly customized 1958 Thunderbird convertible. Her Macabre Mobile, created by George Barris, features a spider web grill, skull and bones hubcaps, and a chain steering wheel with pentagram spokes. It played a prominently role in her 1980s film, *Elvira, Mistress of the Dark.* Neil Preston, courtesy Queen B Productions

unique market niche, their playful persona—all this and more instantly guaranteed that we would never forget these cute little cars. Like Packards, Duesenbergs, and Tuckers before them, some '55–57 Thunderbirds may have temporarily suffered the ignominious fate of sitting soaped-up on Honest John's used car lot in the early 1960s. But it wasn't long before they were rescued and restored to their proper place in automotive Valhalla.

These cars were stars even before they first began joining up with pop culture forces in the 1960s, meaning a quick trip to immortality was made even easier. Once preserved forever in song and on the silver screen, the Thunderbird legend achieved a wider scope—a mass appeal for more casual observers who otherwise may have never considered it possible for a car to become a pop icon.

Soon to be icons themselves, the Beach Boys first turned to Dearborn's two-seater for lyrical inspiration in 1963. When songwriter Brian Wilson needed a measuring stick to demonstrate the rubber-burning prowess of a '32 Ford hot rod he chose a T-Bird. "Just a Little Deuce Coupe with a flathead mill," crooned the Wilson brothers and friends. "But she'll walk a Thunderbird like it's standing still." Who cared that a T-Bird really wasn't that hot of a car? Girl- and boy-crazy Beach Boys fans never noticed—they truly didn't "know what I got"—nor did they care. Most of them never set foot on a surfboard, either.

What the fans did know was how to have loads of fun, at least until "daddy took the T-Bird away." The Beach Boy's 1964 hit single, *Fun, Fun, Fun,* better reflected the Thunderbird's place in the cool world. A performance reputation was purely the product of mirrors. Status, prestige, and pizzazz, on the other hand, were all proven quantities. In this instance Wilson hit the nail right on the head. A two-seat T-Bird was the perfect rich man's toy, whether the playmate in question was a daughter, a wife, or a mistress.

This classy chassis image was perfect for both movies and television. A red two-seat T-Bird fit Robert Urich like a glove for his role as detective Dan Tanna in ABC's "Vegas," aired from 1978 to 1981. Sexy assistants, life-in-the-fast-lane Las Vegas nights, and a too-cool-for-school Thunderbird—what else could a man want?

In Curt Henderson's case, the answer to that question came in the form of a '56 Thunderbird. Easily the most renowned starring role for a T-Bird came in George Lucas' 1973 hit movie *American Graffiti,* when Henderson, played by Richard Dreyfuss, stumbles upon the perceived love of his life, Suzanne Somers, while cruising the strip the night before he is to fly off east to college. "The most perfect, dazzling creature I've ever seen" continues to taunt Henderson from her virgin white T-Bird right up to the movie's end.

Whether she was the young trophy wife of a wealthy jeweler or a high-priced call girl mattered not at all. "I just saw a vision, I saw a goddess," was Curt's claim. But would he have been equally dazzled had Somers been riding in the backseat of a '58 Edsel four-door like him?

Four-place Thunderbirds, to a lesser degree, also became cogs in Hollywood's image machine. On television, Paul Drake, Perry Mason's soft-spoken, broad-shouldered private investigator, drove a Squarebird convertible with style and flair on the rare occasions when he wasn't standing around Mason's office taking up space. Another Squarebird later accompanied Elvira, Mistress of the Dark, in the 1980s, if only because it could be customized so easily to reflect its own dark side. Who was looking at the car though?

Poor little rich boy Robert Conrad showed little respect for his Roundbird convertible while playing bump and run with Troy Donahue in the 1963 film *Palm Springs Weekend.* But Conrad's destructive driving paled in comparison to what Geena Davis and Susan Sarandon did to a '66 T-Bird droptop in the 1991 movie *Thelma and Louise.* Just because the name was Thunderbird didn't mean the car could fly.

Fortunately, the T-Bird legacy hasn't suffered the same fate. Like Elvis, it will never die, not as long as art continues to perpetuate life.

Chapter 3

A Really Big Show
1967-1979

Without a doubt, the Thunderbird tale ranks as one of the most diverse, if not disjointed, in American automotive history. To say the T-Bird lineage has featured many different cars for many different drivers is an understatement. One-time rival Corvette has managed to stay on the road for as long as it has by doing one thing really well. It was, is, and always will be, "America's sports car." Thunderbird, on the other hand, has owed its lengthy career to Ford's frequent willingness to make alterations. Surviving for 43 model runs in a marketplace full of fickle car buyers was a matter of adaptability. Change, sometimes radical, sometimes subtle, was a T-Bird trademark from the beginning.

Purists can stomp their feet all they want in reference to the original two-seater's all-too-short career. If Dearborn designers had not widened the T-Bird's

'Bird watchers who thought Ford had gone one step beyond in 1958 were jolted again in 1967. Adding two more places was one thing. Two more doors really changed all the rules.

appeal by doubling its seating capacity, the legacy undoubtedly would have ended right then and there—three years and out. Unlike Chevrolet, Ford simply wasn't willing to continue pouring its best efforts into a project that could only offer a return of 15,000 to 20,000 unit sales a year. Market realities ruled the auto industry. Keeping the Thunderbird flying beyond 1957 meant more was in order. More car. More riders. More sales.

But if Thunderbird followers were shocked when Ford added two more seats in 1958, they had another surprise coming in 1967. Luxury was still the Thunderbird's main attraction, but it was no longer so personal. Not even close. Times had clearly changed and the totally new fifth-generation Thunderbird was rolling proof . . . big rolling proof.

Actually, the 1967 Thunderbird only *appeared* larger than life. Its imposing image overshadowed specification realities. Styling chiefs David Ash and Bill Boyer saw to that by sculpting a thoroughly modern, angular body featuring lines that looked longer, lower, and wider than they really were. At 115 inches, the wheelbase was only two clicks longer than the 1966 model. The overall length also compared closely, 205.4 inches for 1966 against 206.9 inches for 1967. The overall width was the same. And as bulky as the 1967 'Bird appeared to the eye, in truth it weighed, almost amazingly, less than its

What a difference a year makes. In 1966, Ford built the last Thunderbird convertible. In 1967, the four-door Landau hardtop debuted as sexy sportiness was exchanged for status-conscious plushness. Dig those suicide doors in back.

forerunners—amazingly because at a glance the fifth-generation Thunderbird looked like twice the car in comparison to the 1966.

This apparent violation of physical laws can be explained by what lay beneath that seemingly expansive skin. The unitized body construction used from 1958 to 1966 was traded for a traditional full frame in 1967. Sure, that frame was reinforced with extra weight-gaining members to guarantee a quiet, sure ride. And the 1967 bodyshell itself was also beefed to help meet those ends. Yet the entire battleship-steady package—as rigid and roomy as it was—still weighed less than what came before, because unitized construction required a significant amount of body bracing to make up for the lack of a true frame. Cost cutting also played a role in the decision to switch back to body-on-frame construction—a unitized body was more expensive to manufacture.

The 1967 Thunderbird's excellent ride was also enhanced by a return to coil-spring suspension for the rear wheels, something earlier T-Birds had briefly used in 1958 only. Two-seat 'Birds and those built between 1959 and 1966 had all used parallel leaf springs in back.

New-for-1967 features, along with that palatial body, included trendy hideaway headlights. Up front, the 1967 Thunderbird was all grille. In back, it was all taillight. And down the bodysides it looked like it was all wheel, even though rim diameter, at 15 inches, remained a carryover from 1966. Full, semicircular rear wheel openings contributed to this effect due to both their definitely enlarged size and the fact they weren't enclosed by fender skirts, as had been a T-Bird practice from the outset in 1955.

The really big news for 1967, however, involved the Thunderbird's revised model lineup. In place of the deep-sixed convertible bodystyle came a new four-door sedan, a definite departure from the previously popularized personal luxury theme. Ford officials were especially proud of this break from the existing T-Bird ideal. Promotional paperwork played up the car's newfound place in Ford Motor Company's prestigious pecking order. "Heretofore, a buyer of Ford products had no place to go between the Mercury Park Lane and the Lincoln Continental," explained Ford's 1967 sales book. "Now he has Thunderbird."

Two extra doors—mounted in rearward-hinged "suicide" fashion—were an appropriate addition for this fresh brand of T-Bird status, at least in Ford men's minds. Others were not so easily impressed. "The idea of adding two more doors to the T-Bird is being treated like the invention of the cotton gin by Ford, but the change is hardly worth the hoopla," claimed a *Car and Driver* review.

Customers apparently thought differently. Production of the 1967 four-door Landau sedan (which rolled on a lengthened 117-inch wheelbase) reached 24,967. Compare that figure to the 1966 Thunderbird convertible's 5,049 production total and you begin to get the picture. Sales success talked, diminishing images

Trendy hideaway headlights became a Thunderbird feature for the first time in 1967.

walked. Clearly, trading sexy sportiness for prestigious practicality proved to be the wise move, slings and arrows from early 'Bird devotees notwithstanding.

The Thunderbird's fifth generation, per Ford tradition, lasted three years. Production was 77,956 in 1967, then the third highest total in T-Bird history. Additional highlights of the 1967–69 run included the addition of a standard front bench seat in 1968 that upped seating room to six. A 1969 headline-making addition was the introduction of a new standard Thunderbird engine, the 429-cid Thunder Jet V-8. In 1967 and 1968, a 390 FE-series big-block had been standard, with a 428 FE available as an option. In 1969, the only engine available was the new, cleaner-running 385-series 429, rated at 360 horsepower.

Considerably less well known, yet deserving of historical note, were the five "Apollo Thunderbirds" built by Dearborn Steel Tubing in 1967. Home to Ford's Thunderbolt Fairlane factory drag cars of 1964, Dearborn Steel Tubing dressed up these five two-door T-Birds as part of a promotional effort for the renowned Abercrombie & Fitch sporting goods firm. All five were painted metallic Apollo blue with a matching blue vinyl top. A complete list of options was complemented by an electric sun roof and quartz iodine driving lights. Unique touches included blue-chromed wheelcovers, golden Thunderbird grille badges, chromed door jambs, special side marker lights, and exclusive gold-tinted landau bars. Interior luxury was enhanced with, among other things, a radio, telephone, and a Philco television.

Priced at about $15,000, the Apollo Thunderbirds were displayed at Abercrombie & Fitch stores in Miami, Palm Beach, New York, and Chicago. The fifth model, intended for San Francisco, was destroyed on the way west. According to the International Thunderbird Club, at least two of the Apollo Thunderbirds have survived and are in collectors' hands.

Back in the regular-production world, a sixth-generation Thunderbird debuted in 1970, the product of the presence of short-term Ford President Semon "Bunkie" Knudsen, a General Motors defector who had brought much GM-style thinking to Dearborn when he had jumped across the fence in February 1968. Way too much of a mover and shaker for Henry Ford II's taste, Bunkie was quickly fired in September 1969, but not before he had been able to make a few changes. One of these involved adding a Pontiac-style "beak" to the Thunderbird that alone lengthened the car by six inches.

Like Bunkie Knudsen, the sixth-generation T-Bird was not well received and only lasted two years. After 50,364 were sold in 1970, production dropped like a rock to 36,055 in 1971, a signal that yet another change was in order.

Although some critics applauded the 1967 T-Bird's interior for the way it toned down the "airplane-pilot syndrome" common to earlier models, the driver's position still resembled an aircraft cockpit, thanks mostly to its large, wraparound console. In 1967, the Swing-Away steering wheel became a Tilt-Away as it moved to the side and tilted up to allow easy access.

The one-millionth Thunderbird was built at Ford's Pico Rivera plant in Los Angeles on June 22, 1972. After being used for a year by the Classic Thunderbird Club International's best of show winner, it was purchased by collector George Watts. Bob Peterson bought the car from Watts in 1985. *Bob Peterson*

With Lee Iacocca now in the top seat at Ford (since 1970), the Thunderbird was treated to a complete makeover for 1972 to undo what Bunkie had done. Iacocca's 'Bird would end up being the largest yet, thanks to the fact that it shared the Lincoln Continental Mk IV's platform. The seventh-generation Thunderbird, a luxury showboat to say the least, rolled out on a truly long 120.4-inch wheelbase. The overall length was an aircraft-carrier-like 216 inches, while the total width was 79.3 inches.

With weight also increased, Ford engineers in 1972 introduced a new optional V-8 for the Thunderbird, a 460-cubic-inch monster that shoved aside the Squarebird's old 430 to become the largest T-Bird engine ever offered. Net output rating for the low-compression 460 big-block was 224 horsepower, compared to 212 horses for the standard 429 V-8.

The year also marked a return to a singular model offering since the four-door sedan was dropped. Roomier and more luxurious than ever before, the 1972 two-door Thunderbird brought buyers back into the fold in impressive fashion. Sales that year soared by nearly 70 percent over 1971's results to 57,814. Another 87,269 Lincoln-'Birds were sold in 1973, a new third-place sales standard for the Thunderbird heritage.

Ford had sold its one-millionth Thunderbird the year before, an event that didn't go by unnoticed. A special photo opportunity, complete with an obligatory banner, was arranged as the car rolled off the Los Angeles assembly line on June 22, 1972. Special touches to the car itself included custom gold paint set off by a white vinyl roof and white leather seats. Unique cast-bronze medallions identifying this 460-powered T-Bird as the "Millionth Thunderbird, 1955–1972" were added to the landau bars. And it was the only T-Bird produced in 1972 with white bodyside moldings.

After serving temporary duty as a prize for the Best of Show winner at the Classic Thunderbird Club International's 1972 convention, the one-millionth Thunderbird was sold to Californian George Watts, the same man who still owns the 1955 T-Bird that carries serial number 0005. In 1985, Watts sold the car to its present owner, Bob Peterson, of Cedar Rapids, Iowa.

The Thunderbird's 20th birthday arrived three years after the one-millionth T-Bird came and went, and Ford apparently had exhausted all its celebratory efforts in June 1972. No specific 20th Anniversary model was concocted; basically all 1975 Thunderbirds were considered commemorative editions. Two new appearance options were offered midyear for 1975, but such status-conscious paint and trim packages were nothing new for the biggest 'Birds, which grew even bigger that year as overall length stretched to 225.6 inches. Joining the 1974 Gold and White luxury group options were 1975's Silver and Copper luxury trim groups. Included in these deals were special half-vinyl roofs, seats done in either leather or crushed velour, deluxe wheelcovers, and specially appointed trunks.

The following year was the last for the Continental-based Thunderbirds, and thankfully so in some minds. Rising fuel costs were enough to convince many customers that bigger no longer meant better. Still others were becoming turned off by the overstuffed 'Bird's overdone opulence. In a February 1976 *Motor Trend* article entitled "Farewell to the Big Bird Thunderbird," Tony Swan called the 1976 T-Bird "a Rubenesque leather-padded salon on wheels for middle-class Sybarites."

This commemorative medallion appeared on the millionth Thunderbird's landau bars. Another such medallion was mounted inside on the dash. *Bob Peterson*

All Thunderbirds built in 1975 were considered Twentieth-Anniversary models. Two special trim options—Silver Luxury and Copper Luxury—were also introduced midyear to help mark the moment. A half-vinyl roof complemented the paint finish, as did the windshield—the glass on this Copper Luxury 1975 'Bird is tinted to match exterior color.

Before the last big 'Bird could say farewell, another limited-edition package was created, this one every bit as secretively as Abercrombie & Fitch's blue babies of 1967. In late May 1976, a total of 32 "commemorative" Thunderbirds rolled off the Wixom line. Built for dealer promotions in Charleston, West Virginia, and the Cincinnati-Dayton area, these cars featured silver metallic paint with contrasting black vinyl half-roofs and black leather interiors. Additionally, the American Sunroof Corporation added a special moonroof and a simulated spare tire mount atop the rear deck. Not much is known about these cars; not even Ford officials can answer questions about them since they were promotional products inspired from outside the company, not from within.

Thunderbirds built between 1972 and 1976 were as plush on the inside as they were big all over. Here, the Copper Luxury trim treatments carry over into the passenger compartment as well.

The bigger-must-be-better trend reversed itself after 1976. By then, huge, heavy cars with equally huge appetites for fuel and heavy bottom lines would no longer cut it in the American market. The Thunderbird was no exception. Just 10 years before, growth had been the key to the breed's continued success. In 1977, the opposite became true in a big way.

The debut of the eighth generation represented the first time a new Thunderbird rolled out in smaller form than the car it replaced. At 114 inches, the 1977 T-Bird's wheelbase was 6 inches shorter than the 1976 showboat's. Overall length dropped a whopping 17 inches, while weight went from about 5,000 pounds to

around 4,000. Engine size went down, too—a 302-cid small-block V-8 came under that long hood unless a customer paid more for a 351 or 400.

Though still appearing reasonably large to the eye, the latest Thunderbird was now a mid-sized model clearly based on Ford's LTD II platform. It also now wore a midsized window sticker coming in at about $2,700 less than 1976's prices. Therein was the key to the all-new 1977 Thunderbird's success.

Easier to buy, easier to keep fueled, easier to handle, even easier on the eye, the eighth-generation Thunderbird soared where no T-Bird had gone before. The previous sales record, 92,843 in 1960,

Ford marked its 75th year in 1978 with this special Diamond Jubilee Thunderbird model, which featured a long list of standard dress-up touches like a half-vinyl roof and turbine-style aluminum wheels. Exterior shades were either Diamond Blue Metallic or Ember Metallic.

wasn't just broken, it was obliterated. Production in 1977 hit 318,140, a sixfold increase over 1976's final tally. Thunderbird sales reached their zenith the following year, finishing at 352,751. Results for 1979, though down to "only" 284,141, still stand at almost twice the next highest model-year for sales.

Highlights from this incredibly successful three-year run included the introduction of a sporty "T-roof" option in the spring of 1978. That year also brought a special Diamond Jubilee model to help commemorate Ford's 75th birthday. With a price tag of $10,106, the 1978 Diamond Jubilee T-Bird was called "the most exclusive Thunderbird you can buy." An extensive list of special touches included a monochromatic exterior done in either diamond blue metallic or ember metallic paint, a matching padded vinyl roof, unique trim, and color-keyed aluminum "turbine" wheels. Inside was a leather-wrapped steering wheel, a

A suitably plush interior featuring unique "Biscuit" cloth upholstery typically complemented the Diamond Jubilee Thunderbird's exterior. The instrument panel and steering wheel both included leather coverings.

leather-covered dash, simulated ebony wood treatments, and a 22-karat gold-plated owner's nameplate, to name just a few of the special features.

In 1979 a similar topline package, the Heritage Edition, was offered. Again, the exterior was monochromatic with matching turbine wheels. Color choices were maroon or light blue. The quickest way to identify a Heritage Edition T-Bird in 1979 was by the absence of rear quarter windows. Many of the same Diamond Jubilee trim treatments and such were also included in the Heritage Edition's equally

long list of standard features. As in 1978, owners in 1979 could also put their initials on one of these prestigious Thunderbirds by way of an exclusive plaque.

All this glitter and pizzazz demonstrated that the Thunderbird legacy remained primarily one of luxury, even if the car itself had been dropped down out of Ford Motor Company's most posh ranks into the reach of the masses. Sure, the 1977–79 models were gussied-up LTD IIs. But they were still Thunderbirds.

Diamond Jubilee treatments even extended to the car's trunk.

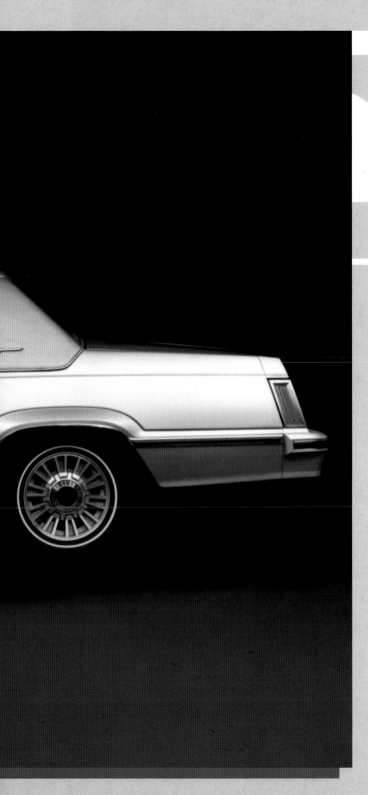

Chapter 4

Bye-Bye, Birdie—for Now

1980-1997

By 1980 Ford had sold more than 2 million Thunderbirds in a wide array of shapes and sizes: sporty two-seater, comfortable four-place cruiser, luxurious showboat with doors for as many as four, full-blown cruise ship, and midsized mass-market marvel. These were Thunderbirds all, vast disparities notwithstanding. With a new decade, however, came a new continuity. While the T-Bird shape would change three more times before the string ran out in 1997, the size would remain similar for the next 2 million 'Birds to follow after 1980.

More downsizing arrived that year, coming at a time when Ford was marketing the Thunderbird through its luxury

A redesigned, downsized Thunderbird emerged to mark the breed's quarter-century anniversary in 1980. Specifically commemorating 25 years of T-Birds was the Silver Anniversary model, introduced that spring. As before, a padded half-vinyl roof once again crowned the Thunderbird's latest flagship. *Ford Motor Company*

Following hot on the heels of the disappointing ninth-generation Thunderbird was Jack Telnack's aero coupe, introduced for 1983. This thoroughly modern bodyshell proved to be a real winner, especially so on NASCAR racetracks. Shown here is the upscale Heritage rendition of the 1983 Thunderbird. Special identification and a more plush interior marked the Heritage model.

image. However, a truly new and youthful impression was around the corner for the more mechanically-conscious sports coupes of 1983–88 and 1989–97. Differences did set the last three Thunderbird generations apart, but the trio shared the same targeted market—family types who like to ride head and shoulders above the mundane in a flashy, easy-to-handle midsized car wearing a not-so-flashy midsized price tag.

The same market pressures that in 1977 had reversed the Thunderbird's rise into Ford's elite luxury stratosphere remained strong as the 1980s dawned. A new accountability was required. Buyers needed affordable, practical cars that did more than just wow the neighbors and look impressive parked in front of the country club. Pizzazz, prestige, and performance were still valued, but so too was fuel economy, convenience, and comfort—that meant a place for the kids, too.

Readjusted thinking at Ford helped usher in the latest redesigned Thunderbird in 1980. It was based on the Fox-chassis platform, itself introduced beneath Ford's Fairmont and Mercury's Zephyr in 1978. Choosing the Fox platform meant a return to unitized body/frame construction for the Thunderbird after rolling on a full frame for 13 years.

In Thunderbird garb, the Fox chassis was stretched slightly, yet the 1980 T-Bird still measured 17 inches shorter than its 1977–79 forerunner and it weighed 700 pounds less. The wheelbase was now 108.4 inches and total length was 200.4 inches. The car was compact-looking to say the least, an impression enhanced even further by Jack Telnack's all-new angular, boxy styling. Although definitely crisp and fresh when first seen, the look quickly turned sour in naysayers' minds. As did the entire car.

In many opinions, the 1980–82 years are called the least memorable of the Thunderbird legacy. Then again, there never has been a shortage of sharply divided subjective viewpoints in the T-Bird arena, and every model group after 1957 taken pokes for one reason or another–some

The Thunderbird Turbo Coupe was instantly identified in 1983 by its unique front fascia (with foglamps) and 14-inch aluminum wheels wearing P205/70HR performance rubber. Turbo Coupes were offered up through 1988. *Ford Motor Company*

The heart of the Turbo Coupe was a 2.3-liter overhead-cam four-cylinder with electronic fuel injection and a Garrett AIResearch T-03 turbocharger. The maximum output for this force-fed four was 145 horsepower at 5,000 rpm. *Ford Motor Company*

1980–82 T-Bird was trendy. Unfortunately, the trend it followed–like that whole disco thing–didn't age well.

Making matters worse was the engineering. At the time Detroit was still having difficulties catching up with federal government demands to clean up its act. The automakers needed to lower engine emissions while at the same time maximizing efficiency to keep up with rising fuel prices. Many powerplants of the early 1980s were still suffering from leaned-out, choked-up, low-compression 1970s-style maladies since electronic computer controls had yet to arrive in force to save the day.

The 1980 Thunderbird was no exception. Its new standard V-8 was a 4.2-liter (255 cid), with the 302 small-block as an option. While both V-8s offered improved fuel economy (partly because they had less weight to lug around) compared to the relative gas-guzzlers that came before, they suffered considerably in the muscle department. Net output for the 255 was 115 horsepower; 131 for the 302.

If that wasn't enough to douse your fire, Ford even introduced an optional six-cylinder–a first for the Thunderbird family–very late in 1980. This wimpy 3.3-liter (200-cid) inline-six produced an underwhelming 88 horsepower. And to add insult to injury, in 1981 it became the T-Bird's standard engine. It was joined in 1982 by another six-holer, the 112 horsepower 3.8-liter (232-cid) V-6. The 302 V-8 was dropped that year, leaving only the optional 255 for buyers trying to remember the days when the "Thunder" in Thunderbird actually meant something.

much more than others. Until the downsized, four-place Thunderbird came along in 1980, the easiest targets had been the big 'Birds of 1967–71 and the even bigger renditions that followed.

Critics of the 1980–82 era commonly complain about blah styling that echoed a blah moment in American automotive history. Ford wasn't alone. So many of Detroit's offerings in those days looked like bricks on wheels. If anything, the

The FILA Thunderbird was created in 1984 as part of a joint effort with Italy's FILA Sports, Incorporated, an activewear manufacturer. The car's paint, lower body black-out, monochromatic wheels and trim, and pinstriping were all part of the exclusive package. *Ford Motor Company*

Setting aside any and all opinions about styling, it was what came beneath the skin of the 1980–82 T-Bird that probably sealed its fate. Engineering aspects alone left critics shaking their heads—and buyers closing their checkbooks. Thunderbird sales looked fine in 1980, even though they finished well short of 1979's sky-high results. But after 156,803 1980 'Birds rolled off dealership lots, only 86,693 were sold in 1981. The story got even worse the following year when the total for 1982 Thunderbirds fell to 45,142.

At least this generation was able to record one major claim to fame. Its first year, of course, was the Thunderbird's 25th on the road. And Ford couldn't let that moment pass without putting together a special Silver Anniversary model. Exclusive Silver Anniversary paint (other solid colors and two-tone arrangements were also offered), eye-catching cast-aluminum wheels, simulated-wood dash appointments, and a leather-wrapped steering wheel were just a few of the features included. Most agreed the Silver Anniversary Thunderbird was an impressive package, but once the party was over, the T-Bird crowd found little reason to celebrate in 1981 and 1982. This may well have been one time when three years and out was probably the right choice.

Telnack's design team came to the rescue in 1983 with the "Aerobird." Actually another downsized model, although you

The highly successful tenth-generation Thunderbird hit the streets for the last time in 1988, ending a six-year stretch where production tallies never fell below 128,000. The peak year for the Aerobird was 1984 when 170,533 were sold. This 1988 'Bird is one of 147,243 built that year.

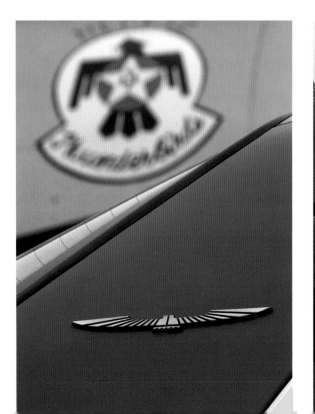

couldn't really tell at a glance, the 1983 Thunderbird was based on a revised Fox chassis with a shortened 104-inch wheelbase. Overall impressions, however, left most witnesses seeing very little difference between the 1983 and 1982 T-Birds as far as exterior dimensions were concerned–from a curbside perspective, that is. Once inside, however, rear seat passengers quickly discovered the car's reduced nature since their space was sacrificed in order to keep driver comfort up to 1980–82 standards.

The overall length and width also decreased, all as part of a fresh, new "high-tech" plan to help the updated 10th-generation T-Bird cut through the wind like no Thunderbird ever did. Slighted by some as a "jellybean," Telnack's cutting-edge body featured an exceptional 0.35 drag coefficient–great by performance car standards, even greater in a machine many looked to for hauling the kids and family dog around town.

While the aero coupe look revived the Thunderbird's sagging image, its mechanicals remained disappointing. At first. The 3.8-liter V-6 was the base engine in 1983, but it was soon rejoined by the 302 V-8, an option added midyear. Yet another midyear performance addition really got things rolling.

With its new slippery shell, the 1983 Thunderbird was a natural for the sporty crowd. Once the Turbo Coupe was introduced in April 1983, the package was complete. Sure, the heart of the Turbo Coupe was *only* a four-cylinder engine. But this four-banger was fitted with a Garrett

AIResearch turbocharger that helped squeeze out an amazing 145 horsepower from 2.3 liters. Included in the Turbo Coupe deal was a five-speed manual transmission, a 3.45:1 Traction-Lok differential, and a special handling package incorporating "Quadra-shocks" out back.

"Three decades later, the T-Bird finally becomes what it started out to be," wrote *Motor Trend's* Ron Grable concerning the 1983 Turbo Coupe. Though it didn't quite qualify as a muscle car, the turbocharged T-Bird did represent a very nice compromise between luxury–could that have been *personal* luxury?–and performance.

And if you thought the 1983 version was trick, you couldn't help but love the 1987 Turbo Coupe. With dual exhausts and an intercooler, turbo-four output increased to 190 horsepower. Four-wheel discs with ABS, automatic ride control, and 16-inch wheels were also added. *Motor Trend* editors liked it so much they named the 1987 Turbo Coupe their "Car of the Year." Turbo Coupes remained popular throughout the 10th generation's six-year run, which ended in 1988.

All of Ford's aero coupe Thunderbirds from 1983 to 1988 were strong sellers, a situation not hurt in the least by the car's rapid rise to the top of NASCAR's Winston Cup racing scene. Healthy production runs ranged from a low of 121,999 in 1983 to a peak of 170,533 in 1984. Even with its replacement waiting in the wings, the 1988 T-Bird still attracted 147,868 customers. In 1985, when 151,851 models were sold, Ford once again marked a special moment, this time with a 30th-Anniversary model.

Features included Regatta blue clearcoat metallic paint, unique bodyside moldings, and an exclusive exterior tape treatment.

Considering how much drivers appreciated the 1983–88 Thunderbird, it was obvious that its successor would have to be some special car . . . and it was. Donald Petersen's team at Ford reportedly spent $1 billion trying to upstage the 10th-generation T-Bird. That cash ended up being very well spent. The last Thunderbird rendition easily stands as the breed's best all-around combination of sportiness, practicality, luxury, and performance–all at a price that might have enticed original T-Bird buyers to come home with two or three.

Initial plans for this car, like those for the next-generation Mustang, which was also in the works, called for a smaller, front-wheel-drive model. In the Thunderbird's case, the platform would come from the wildly popular Taurus/Sable line. Luckily Ford officials changed their minds in both cases. The planned front-drive Mustang became the Probe as Dearborn's revered pony car continued on into the 1990s with rear-wheel drive and V-8 power. As for the T-Bird, it too stayed true to its heritage even as General Motors was reintroducing their competing midsized models on the front-wheel-drive GM10 platform.

To keep the thunder rolling into a fifth decade, Ford engineers created the MN12

An even sleeker Thunderbird body was introduced for 1989 along with independent rear suspension and an optional supercharged V-6. The latter feature came along as part of the Thunderbird SC package, identified here by its lower-body cladding. *Tom Wilson, courtesy of Dobbs Publishing Group*

platform featuring good ol' meat-and-potatoes rear-wheel drive. The big difference, however, came in the way those rear-drive wheels were suspended. Like Corvettes since 1963, the startling 1989 Thunderbird featured independent rear suspension. On top of that, the sleek new body was even more aerodynamic than its Aerobird predecessor. Reportedly, some 700 hours of wind-tunnel testing went into the design, which cheated the wind with a superb 0.31 drag coefficient.

The 1989 Thunderbird was slightly wider and lower than its 1988 forerunner, but it measured 3.4 inches shorter end-to-end, even though the MN12 wheelbase went nine inches beyond the Fox chassis' hub-to-hub stretch. Moving the wheels farther apart meant both ride and rear seat room were greatly enhanced. Most critics also agreed that appearances were enhanced as well. Those long, low lines made the last-generation T-Bird look like it was flying along even as it stood at rest.

If there was one complaint, it involved power choices. A V-8 was not brought back for the 1989 Thunderbird, a fact that many long-time T-Bird buyers repeatedly reminded dealers about. Even though the standard 140 horsepower 3.8-liter V-6 was no slouch, there remained no substitute for cubic inches in most 'Bird fans' minds. A V-8 was still a V-8, and a V-6 wasn't.

But Ford officials didn't turn a deaf ear to customers' clamoring for a truly hot Thunderbird. In place of the absent V-8 model, Dearborn unveiled the 1989 Super Coupe, a certifiably sexy concoction on

Ford marked 35 years of Thunderbird history in 1990 with this anniversary SC model. Monochromatic black with blue striping and silver accents was the exclusive exterior treatment on all Thirty-fifth Anniversary T-Birds. *Ford Motor Company*

The sun went down on the Thunderbird in 1997 after 43 model runs—temporarily, that is. An all-new 'Bird is expected for the new millennium.

looks alone, what with its trendy lower body cladding, fog lamps, and 16x7 cast-aluminum wheels wearing fat Goodyear Eagle rubber.

What really got T-Bird drivers' hearts pumping, however, was the powerplant that hid behind those "SC" letters impressed into the car's lower front fascia. Making the Super Coupe so super was a force-fed 3.8 liter V-6. Supplying 12 pounds of maximum boost, the SC's Eaton supercharger instantly reminded many elder Thunderbird fans of the blown 'Birds of 1957. Only this time the power package included an intercooler and sequential multiport electronic fuel injection, too. All this techno-wizardry translated into 210 horses at the rear wheels. In turn, this

meant the 1989 Super Coupe could trip the lights at the far end of the quarter-mile in about 15.8 seconds–not bad at all for a car that could also turn heads at both the grocery store and the theater.

Also included in the Super Coupe deal were four-wheel ABS disc brakes, a Traction-Lok differential, automatic ride control, and heavy-duty front and rear stabilizer bars. A five-speed manual transmission was standard, with Ford's AOD (automatic-overdrive) transmission also available. Among interior goodies were articulating sport seats (with power lumbar support) and special instrumentation.

Buyers weren't the only ones impressed. "In 1987, when we named the Thunderbird Turbo Coupe our Car of

75

Despite its 40-year run, Ford opted not to mark the Thunderbird's transition from 1955 to 1995 with any exclusive packaging, leaving some dealerships to do the honors with commemorative decals and striping.

the Year, we called it the highest-flying Thunderbird ever produced," announced a 1989 *Motor Trend* report. "Little did we realize as we penned those words that Ford was, at the same moment, preparing a new supercharged vehicle that would take the Thunderbird name closer to the stratosphere."

The exciting 1989 Super Coupe became the third Thunderbird to win *Motor Trend's* "Car of the Year" award. And the SC Thunderbird continued impressing drivers right up to its retirement in 1995, the year the T-Bird celebrated its 40th birthday. Alone. As was the case with the 30th year of Mustang in 1994, Ford officials chose not to release a special commemorative Thunderbird in 1995. Fortunately dealers were willing to pick up the slack, adorning some 1995 T-Birds with 40th Anniversary identification.

Five years earlier, a 35th Anniversary Thunderbird was released by Ford midyear in 1990. It was appropriately based on the SC model and featured black paint with blue striping and a contrasting titanium lower body treatment. Black leather seats and black-painted wheels were also included.

In 1991, customer complaints finally influenced Ford to revive the V-8–powered Thunderbird. A 200 horsepower 5.0-liter V-8 was made an option that year. Three years later, the venerable 5.0 liter-pushrod V-8 was replaced by an optional 205 horsepower 4.6-liter modular V-8. And the Super Coupe in 1994 got a power boost to 230 horsepower thanks to a revised Eaton supercharger with low-drag, Teflon-coated rotors. A Thunderbird

facelift that year also changed appearances slightly at both ends, while the basic shape remained identical.

Dearborn's decision not to officially mark the Thunderbird's 40th anniversary in 1995 was probably a result of the plain fact that the T-Bird's days were already numbered. Although the decision to end the Thunderbird's long, legendary run–albeit temporarily–in 1997 appeared abrupt and somewhat cold-hearted, market realities made it clear in 1989 that an end was in sight. Proof began to appear once it became obvious that Ford had no plans to bring out another new Thunderbird in the 1990s, instead opting to continue production, year in, year out, of basically the same car through nine nearly identical model runs.

Then, after all those years and all those cars, Dearborn also chose not to bid the final 1997 Thunderbird a fond farewell. Not even a typical press release photo appeared. According to one Lorain, Ohio, source, the historic moment was marked only by "a quiet affair for the plant workers." Of course, Ford people chose to skip a long goodbye because they didn't want this to appear as a dead end. "The Thunderbird will return by the turn of the century," was the word from Ford by way of convenient press leaks. What form the new Thunderbird will take remains, as this is being written, the $64,000 question.

The biggest question asked by Thunderbird devotees in 1997 is, why did the existing coupe have to be grounded a few years short of the new 'Bird's introduction?

The very last Thunderbird built, shown here, rolled off Ford's Lorain assembly plant on September 4, 1997. It was then donated to the Classic Thunderbird Club International in Southern California.

The answer involves Ford plans to cut back on the number of vehicle platforms offered worldwide. It has been common knowledge for some time that Ford's rear-wheel-drive platform for the Thunderbird and Mercury Cougar wouldn't survive into the new millennium. With the rug pulled out from under it, the Thunderbird simply wasn't going to be allowed to fly on in stopgap fashion until its replacement made its debut.

Besides, by 1993 the handwriting was already on the wall as sales dropped off each year thereafter, considerably so after 1995. The T-Bird essentially drove itself into the ground after Dearborn had clearly thrown in the towel in the early 1990s. As Ford Division Public Affairs

Chief Jim Bright explained, "It's tough and very costly to come out with something new every three or four years." In turn, it also became tough for customers to warm up to what was basically a slightly altered remake of the previous year's model.

But that's all "chicken or egg" stuff. Plain marketing truths were the real culprits behind the move to temporarily retire the Thunderbird badge. Product planners chose not to tinker with the T-Bird in the 1990s because they had eyes. Calling two-door coupe customers "a very fickle lot," Jim Bright pointed to declining sales as the obvious reason for the retirement. In 1977, the T-Bird's share of the total car market had been a healthy 2.9 percent. Model-year sales reached their peak the following year. Then came a rapid drop-off, a trend that not even the 1989 'Bird could turn back. The 11th generation's best model-year performance came in 1993 when 133,109 Thunderbirds were sold. By 1996, total market share had fallen to a dismal 0.9 percent.

Why the sales decline? Because the car's playing field itself was on the decline. During the Thunderbird's 1970s heyday, the midsized specialty car segment made up as much as 12.2 percent (in 1976) of the total vehicle market. By 1989, that chunk had receded to 3.9 percent, and measured only 1.9 in 1996. Thunderbird wasn't alone rolling downhill; it was also joined by Chevrolet's Monte Carlo and Pontiac's Grand Prix.

Even a blind man today can see why the two-door specialty coupe has been

Ford's final Thunderbird is identified by this data plate beneath the hood. By the time you read this, the T-Bird will already be reborn.

squeezed out of Detroit's scheme of things. "A greater number of customers are now turning to light trucks instead of cars," Bright said. "Two-door coupes used to be familiar to family types in the market for utility and versatility."

The 1997 T-Bird remained an affordable, attractive package, but it never had a chance against the ever popular modern-day pickup, and even less against its wildly popular sport-utility derivative. As the 1990s wind down, SUVs continue turning the heads of many customers who earlier might have considered the specialty coupe market.

With SUVs running away with the affections of more and more car buyers, the choice became clear. Ford simply let

Chevrolet and Pontiac have the ever shrinking piece of the midsized specialty pie to themselves. Pontiac's efforts to stave off the inevitable included creating a four-door Grand Prix, a tactic Dearborn never seriously considered. "Naturally we didn't want to compete against ourselves," said Bright.

Ford of course also never considered dropping the Thunderbird nameplate, considering how much this high-flying heritage has meant to the company for 40-something years now. You may already have read about the all-new T-Bird before you picked up this little book. Or maybe you've seen advance photos of it in print.

How does it look?

High-Flying Thunderbirds

The sky has always been the limit for automotive design-ers, especially so in the late 1940s and 1950s when aircraft-inspired fantasies seemed to dominate Detroit's drawing boards. A prime example was the new Cadillac for 1948, a trend-setting showboat that featured those curious little tailfins atop each rear quarter. Legendary designer Frank Hershey, then working under General Motors Styling Chief Harley Earl, was the man behind those fins. The inspiration for Hershey's work? None other than Lockheed's twin-tail P-38 fighter plane of World War II.

Of course, Hershey also supervised the shaping of Ford's high-flying two-seater, a car that borrowed its well-deserved name from a Native American legend that told of a grand bird that ended drought by bringing on thunder and lightning with the flap of its great wings. By coincidence, that glorious name, "Thunderbird," had already been chosen by another group to honor its vehicles for the way they performed so majestically in the heavens.

On May 25, 1953, U.S. Air Force officials activated the 3600th Air Demonstration Team out of Lukes Air Force Base in Arizona. The mission for the 3600th, the "Thunderbirds," was to prove just how reliable and safe the USAF's jet fighters were. Examples of this new technology—Lockheed's F-80 Shooting Star (America's first operational fighter jet), Repub-lic's F-84 Thunderjet, and North American's unbeatable F-86 Sabre—had already demonstrated how well an Air Force jet could fight. The proof came in the skies over Korea beginning in 1950. With that conflict now over, the job became one of continued readiness and demonstrating how well both planes and pilots could perform.

Forty-five years after its inception, the Thunderbirds team has shown its precision-flying prowess before more than 287 million observers in all 50 states, as well as 59 foreign coun-tries. Those beautiful red, white, and blue aircraft have put on more than 3,400 air shows, with not one performance ever canceled for mechanical reasons.

The Thunderbirds team began using the F-16 Fighting Falcon in 1983. Today they fly the upgraded F-16C. *Kevin J. Gruenwald, courtesy Thunderbirds USAF Air Demonstration Squadron, Nellis Air Force Base, Nevada*

Today's Thunderbirds fly the USAF's most versatile fighter, the General Dynamics F-16C Fighting Falcon. Six Fighting Falcons make up the squadron, which performs in precise formations and high-speed solo exhibitions. The latter shows off the F-16's maximum "performance envelope," while multi-aircraft flights, such as the famous four-plane diamond, allow the pilots to parade their exemplary discipline and meticulous training. Lasting about one hour and fifteen minutes, a typical Thunderbirds show features its most active pilot making approximately 30 maneuvers. The unit performs no more than 88 air demonstrations a year between March and November. The winter months are used for new pilot training.

The Thunderbirds Air Combat Command unit actually includes 8 pilots, 4 support officers, 4 civilians, and 130 enlisted people. About half of all personnel are replaced each year. Officers serve a two-year assignment and enlisted members serve three to four years.

Objectives for all these men and women are clear. They include: supporting USAF recruiting and retention programs; reinforcing public confidence in the Air Force and demonstrating the professional competence of Air Force crews; strengthening morale and esprit de corps among Air Force personnel; supporting Air Force community relations; representing the United States and its armed forces to foreign nations; and projecting international goodwill. In 1996, the Thunderbirds squadron did a nine-country, 30-day deployment in Europe. Included were the former communist countries of Romania, Slovenia, and Bulgaria. After returning stateside, the team did a flyover to help open the Atlanta Olympics in July. An estimated 3.8 billion people witnessed that televised performance worldwide.

Thunderbirds performances have featured various Air Force jets over the years, beginning with the straight-winged F-84G Thunderjet in 1953. Republic's improved swept-wing F-84F Thunderstreak became the jet of choice early in 1955. More than 9 million spectators at 222 air shows in North and South America saw the F-84 perform in red, white, and blue regalia.

In 1956, the Thunderbirds team moved to its present home at Nellis Air Force Base in Nevada. That year the team also traded the F-84 for North American's F-100 Super Sabre, the world's first supersonic fighter. More than 1,100 demonstrations were flown using F-100C and F-100D models up into 1969. For six brief shows in 1964, the Thunderbirds squadron used Republic's F-105B Thunderchief before turning to the F-100D.

From 1969 to 1973, the team used the Air Force's latest frontline fighter, the McDonnell-Douglas F-4E Phantom II. Phantoms were featured at more than 500 air shows. Then, to cut costs, the Thunderbirds in 1974 traded the big F-4 for the much smaller, more fuel-efficient Northrop T-38A Talon—the world's first supersonic jet trainer. A two-seat variant of Northrop's popular F-5 Freedom Fighter, the T-38 flew almost 600 demonstrations for the Thunderbirds team, including a flyover at the opening of the National Air and Space Museum in Washington, D.C., in 1976.

Early in 1983, the Thunderbirds squadron returned to "frontline status," dropping the little Talon in favor of the F-16A Fighting Falcon. More than 16.5 million people in 33 states saw the Thunderbirds fly the F-16 that first year. Additional memorable performances included a flyby during the Statue of Liberty rededication on the Fourth of July in 1986 and a trip to China in 1987, which was the first time an American demonstration squadron performed in a communist country. Five years later, the team upgraded to the F-16C.

To see the Thunderbirds perform in the air is as easy as contacting an Air Force base near you for the year's schedule. To see nostalgic examples of former Thunderbirds performers, you might consider visiting the Octave Chanute Aerospace Museum, located on the grounds of the defunct Chanute AFB in Rantoul, Illinois. There you'll find red, white, and blue representatives of both the straight- and swept-wing F-84, the F-100 Super Sabre, the T-38 Talon, the F-16, and even the F-105 "Thud." Only the F-4 is not represented.

For information about the Octave Chanute Aerospace Museum itself, located at 1011 Pacesetter Drive in Rantoul, call (217) 893-1613. Museum hours are 10 A.M. to 5 P.M. weekdays (closed on Tuesdays), Saturday 10 A.M. to 6 P.M., and Sunday noon to 5 P.M. Thunderbird fans are always welcome.

Chapter 5

Battling 'Birds:
A Proud Competition Heritage

Ford's decision to shoot down the Thunderbird in 1997 did more than just disappoint a loyal following on Mainstreet U.S.A. It also left NASCAR's various Blue Oval racing teams wondering where they were going to find a ride.

The midsized T-Bird had carried the Ford banner proudly around stock-car racing's premier circuit since 1978. And it did so especially well in the 1980s in the hands of "Million Dollar" Bill Elliott, who set speed records, won races, and took home winnings like nobody's business. In the 1990s it was underdog Alan Kulwicki and young turk Davey Allison who stepped up to keep the Thunderbird flying high in NASCAR competition.

Extensively lightened through the use of aluminum panels and the deletion of all nonessential items, this not-so-polite two-seater certainly was ready for action, thus its name—"Battlebird." Two such Battlebirds were specially prepared for Daytona Beach's annual Speed Weeks trials. The other car did not survive. Notice the clear aerodynamic covers over the headlights.

Ford originally shipped this T-Bird from Dearborn to DePaolo Engineering in Long Beach, California, in December 1956. There it was transformed from personal luxury cruiser into all-out race car. The aluminum tailfin represented state-of-the-art streamlining for 1957, as did the small plexiglass windscreen.

In July 1997, Ford finally squelched many months' worth of speculation by announcing that the lame duck Thunderbird would be replaced on the 1998 NASCAR scene by, of all things, the Taurus. A four-door NASCAR racer? You got it. And a highly successful one at that. Despite feeble early test results (probably due to sandbagging tactics), NASCAR's first four-door stock car hit the ground running, taking so many top places in the early 1998 races that rules moguls were forced to try to reshape Ford's widely perceived advantage with some mandated rear spoiler adjustments. These changes achieved little. Much of the competition probably wishes the Thunderbird had never left.

Tragedy struck in 1993 when both Ford Motorsports and the entire racing community lost Kulwicki and Allison as each was killed off the track in aviation accidents. They're still dearly missed.

Mark Martin then emerged as Ford's top NASCAR pilot, joined by former Pontiac man Rusty Wallace in 1994. Two years later, Dale Jarrett made his way to the front of the pack. In 1997, Jarrett and Martin kept their T-Birds in the hunt for the Winston Cup championship right up to the season's last race, the NAPA 500 at Atlanta Motor Speedway. The NAPA 500, however, also represented the NASCAR Thunderbird's final fling. And so ended a competition legacy that had produced 184 NASCAR victories since 1978.

The Battlebird's heart was a stroked Y-block, a 348-cube screamer fed by Hilborn injectors. The black stenciled figure on the passenger's side fenderwell represents the last three digits of the car's serial number. This identification is found in various places throughout this factory racing machine.

The Battlebird's interior was completely stripped and refitted with no-nonsense competition gear. Notice the cooling louvers punched into the passenger-side door.

That's not to say the T-Bird was less of a battler on the track. The modern Taurus shell—translated into NASCAR specifications—is just so much better equipped to cheat the wind at superspeedway velocity. Thunderbirds over the years have always been able to ruffle rivals' feathers at competition venues of all kinds, from the hard-packed sands of Daytona Beach and the dangerously loose gravel of Pikes Peak, to the curves of sports car racing's legendary road courses and the blinding salt at Bonneville. Quarter-mile tracks also have been scorched by more than one T-Bird since 1955, with veteran Ford drag racer Bob Glidden turning most heads at the wheel of his Pro Stock 'Bird in the 1980s.

A case of split personality? During their 40-odd years on the street, Thunderbirds were personally prestigious and often luxurious by nature. Yet, at times, they were clearly no strangers to the brutal world of flat-out racing as well. The 1960s and much of the 1970s don't count. Before and after, however, Thunderbird was more than just a name.

Making the jump from mild-mannered motoring to speed-crazed competition in the beginning was no big deal for the two-seat 'Bird. While Ford did play down the sporting side of the original Thunderbird's nature, owners with a real need for speed couldn't overlook the performance potential of such a small car with such a big (for the time) and powerful V-8. As early as

Racing Thunderbirds were on hand for the first running of the Daytona 500 in February 1959. Fritz Wilson's "Museum of Speed" T-Bird has since been fully restored and now resides in the Klassix Auto Museum, located just west of Daytona International Speedway.

February 1955, Thunderbirds were showing up at sports car racing events like the then-young 12-hour endurance classic at Sebring, Florida. Other battle-ready 'Birds also started appearing at regional roundy-round events in 1955 and at newly founded NHRA dragstrips in 1956.

Pure, straight-line speed was the early 'Bird's main claim to fame in the competition arena. Remember, despite being commonly matched up against the Corvette, the two-seat T-Bird was no sports car. No way, no how. Ford people themselves weren't shy about admitting that plain truth, although they had no qualms about announcing Thunderbird speed records as part of their 1956 ad campaign.

Inspiration for those advertisements had come at Daytona Beach that February. So what if Ford's two-seater couldn't match America's sports car on a twisting road course? Its inherently high power-to-weight ratio meant it could head for the top end in every bit as much of a hurry as the Corvette . . . with the right pieces under the hood, that is.

Thunderbirds returned to NASCAR racing in 1978 after an 18-year hiatus. Here, Bobby Allison pilots his Bud Moore 'Bird at Bristol International Raceway in Bristol, Tennessee, in April 1979. Allison finished second that day in the Southeastern 500. *Dorsey Patrick*

In 1956, those underhood "adjustments" came courtesy of speed merchants like Chuck Daigh, who took his over-bored, streamlined Thunderbird to Florida for NASCAR's Speed Week trials. His main competition there was Chevrolet's Corvette team led by Zora Arkus-Duntov. Daigh's T-Bird initially ran faster than Duntov's 'Vette before both cars were disqualified for being too overbored. Daigh returned to the beach with a stock-spec 312 V-8 fed by dual four-barrel carbs and recorded a 88.779-miles-per-hour average for the standing-mile. In the flying-mile, an Andy Hotten–built (he of Dearborn Steel Tubing) Thunderbird ran 134 miles per hour, good for third place. Even before the Atlantic coast sands had settled, Ford hype-masters had already changed the name to "Thunder Beach."

A truly serious Thunderbird team returned to Daytona in 1957 with full, unabashed factory backing from Dearborn. This team featured four cars, each specially prepared by DePaolo Engineering in Long Beach, California. Two were kept relatively stock in appearance, although they were powered by stroked versions of Ford's optional supercharged Y-block V-8. The other pair were treated to major modifications inside and out. These full-blown experimental racing machines were soon known as "Battlebirds."

The Battlebirds were, in 1957 terms, state-of-the-art factory race cars. At DePaolo Engineering, their frames and suspensions were beefed up and the whole package lightened by eliminating the bumpers and trading the stock doors, hoods, trunks, and headlight rims for pieces hammered out of aluminum. One Battlebird was fitted with a big, stroked 430 cid Lincoln V-8. The other was powered by a 312 Y-block stroked to 348 cubic inches.

While the Lincoln-powered Battlebird was later destroyed, its running mate managed to survive the rigors of

Almost forgotten after his long string of championships at the wheel of Chevrolet products is Dale Earnhardt's short career in a NASCAR Thunderbird. "The Intimidator" raced for Bud Moore in 1982 and 1983. Earnhardt and his T-Bird are shown here on the way to finishing fourth in the Winston Western 500, run at Southern California's Riverside International Raceway on November 20, 1983. *Phillip Salazar*

racing, as well as the more typical ravages of time, and presently resides in Bo Cheadle's fabulous Ford performance collection in California. In the early 1990s it was lovingly restored by classic Thunderbird expert Gil Baumgartner, who painstakingly researched every nut and bolt while re-creating the way the #98 Battlebird looked when it took to the beach in February 1957.

Streamlined touches included plexiglas headlight covers, a cutdown racing windscreen, and a big "Buck Rogers" fin running down the rear deck. Beneath the aluminum hood, the 348-cid Y-block was mounted six inches farther back than stock for better weight balance. Headers were added, as was Hilborn fuel injection and a Vertex magneto in place of the stock distributor. A supercharger was also tried along with the injectors at Daytona in 1957.

Since Ford didn't have a four-speed manual transmission for the 1957 Thunderbird, a Jaguar close-ratio four-speed was adapted to the Battlebird's Y-block. A

The sleek Aerobird body also made the Thunderbird a suitable candidate for SCCA road racing, as John Bauer demonstrates in Trans-Am competition at Riverside in September 1983. *Phillip Salazar*

Bill Elliott became "Million Dollar Bill" in 1985 by copping NASCAR's first "Winston Million," an R. J. Reynolds-sponsored cash bonus awarded to the winner of three of the "Big Four" superspeedway races: the Daytona 500, Talladega's Winston 500, Charlotte's World 600, and Darlington's Southern 500. Elliott's sensational 1985 season included 11 victories in all, yet he and his Thunderbird still finished second to Darrell Waltrip for the championship. *Dorsey Patrick*

Halibrand quick-change rear end in back typically allowed a varying choice of final-drive ratios. And horsepower was finally transferred into speed by way of four Halibrand magnesium knock-off wheels.

Cheadle's Battlebird was driven by Chuck Daigh at Daytona in 1957. Danny Eames got the job of piloting its Lincoln-powered running mate. On the beach, Daigh managed an amazing 205-mile-per-hour flying-mile in his brutal 'Bird but

couldn't make the mandatory return pass due to engine problems–a two-way average speed was required to make the record books. Thus, Daigh's impressive one-way run ended up as nothing more than a Speed Week footnote.

At least Eames' Battlebird did take the official flying-mile title (in the Sports Class B-Modified class), averaging 160.356 for the two-way run, better by 30 miles per hour than the second-place

Cadillac-powered Corvette. Eames also scored the best standing-mile acceleration run (for experimental cars) at 98.065 miles per hour. Daigh finished third in this event with 93.065 miles per hour. As for the two other DePaolo Engineering T-Birds, they ran 1-2 in the stock-class sports car flying-mile at 138.755 and 135.313 miles per hour. Again, these speeds topped the competition by a wide margin.

At that point, the sky appeared to be the limit for the Thunderbird. But then came the Automobile Manufacturers Association's so-called ban on factory racing involvement. In the summer of 1957 that decree convinced Ford Division chief Robert McNamara to slam the engineering department's back door shut on such high-powered projects as the Battlebirds. The two beastly T-Birds quickly found their way into private hands, then rolled

Dominating NHRA Winston Pro Stock pilot Bob Glidden chose Ford's new Probe over the redesigned Thunderbird in 1989, primarily due to a perceived disadvantage created by the 1989 'Bird's longer wheelbase. While driving the shorter Aerobird in 1988 (shown here), Glidden romped and stomped his way to his ninth Winston Pro Stock title. He would win his 10th—and fifth straight—with the Probe in 1989. *Donald Farr, courtesy Super Ford magazine, Dobbs Publishing Group*

Leonard Vahsholtz started racing Thunderbirds up Colorado's famed Pikes Peak in 1984 and never looked back, taking the legendary hillclimb's stock-class title in 1986, 1987, and 1988. *Bob Jackson*

into obscurity until old #98 re-emerged some 35 years later, courtesy of Cheadle and Baumgartner.

With Ford "officially" out of sanctioned competition after 1957, it was left to Holman & Moody in Charlotte, North Carolina, to keep the thunder rolling. Soon recognized as Dearborn's unofficial racing wing, the Holman & Moody firm was requested by Ford in 1959 to build a new breed of track-ready T-Birds, this one for NASCAR's stock-car circuit. Six of these beefed-up 'Birds, armed with

350-horsepower 430 Lincoln V-8s, showed up at Bill France's new Daytona International Speedway in February 1959 for the first running of the Daytona 500. One of these cars, Fritz Wilson's #64 "Museum of Speed" entry, survived its competition career and was later restored. Today, it is on display at Daytona's Klassix Auto Museum just west of the Speedway.

On race day in 1959, Johnny Beauchamp's #73 Thunderbird raced to the wire with Lee Petty's Oldsmobile, and was initially called the winner of the first

Thunderbirds have also made their presence felt in drag racing's top fuel ranks. Here, Eric Reed's Funny Car T-Bird lights 'em up at the Mid-South Nationals in 1989. *Bob Plumer, courtesy Drag Racing Memories, Highland Springs, Virginia*

Daytona 500. But after further review, finish-line photography showed Petty's car had actually taken the checkered flag by about two feet, leaving Beauchamp to snatch defeat from the jaws of victory. Two Thunderbirds did later make their way into NASCAR winners' circles that year.

Racing T-Birds, both 1959 leftovers and a few new models, returned to NASCAR tracks in 1960, but none won a race. The arrival of the Roundbird in 1961 signaled a temporary end to the Thunderbird's short, early career in big-time stock-car racing.

That career was revived in 1978, and in glorious fashion to boot. This time cameras weren't required as Bobby Allison drove his #15 Bud Moore Thunderbird first

In 1989, Lyn St. James drove this specially modified Thunderbird to a women's closed speed record of 212.577 miles per hour at Talladega. Power came from an Ernie Elliott-built 377-cubic-inch V-8. *Donald Farr, courtesy Super Ford magazine, Dobbs Publishing Group*

across the line at the Daytona 500 in February on the way to a second-place finish in the Winston Cup Grand National seasonal points race. Obviously, Ford's downsizing of the Thunderbird in 1977 had transformed the proud 'Bird back into a candidate for competition. Unfortunately, continued downsizing in 1980 only put the NASCAR effort in reverse. True speedway glory didn't come until the bricklike 1980–82 Thunderbird was replaced by the sleek Aerobirds in 1983. Bill Elliott scored his first Winston Cup victory that year in a wind-cheating Thunderbird.

Two years later, Elliott and his T-Bird really got hot, taking a record 11 superspeedway wins, including four in a row. Awesome Bill from Dawsonville also

gained a second clever nickname in 1985 by becoming the first Winston Million winner. Million Dollar Bill earned the big prize by winning three of NASCAR's "Big Four" races–the Daytona 500, Talladega 500, and Southern 500. All told, Elliott raked in $2,433,187 in earnings that year, another record.

In 1986, he established a speed standard–212 miles per hour during Talladega 500 qualifying–that still stands, and probably will forever considering the effort NASCAR rules moguls have since made to limit such astronomical top ends. Elliott's record-breaking efforts were finally rewarded with a Winston Cup championship in 1988, the fourth for a Ford driver.

The Thunderbird's final farewell came in November 1997 at Atlanta's NAPA 500. While Dale Jarrett (number 88) and Mark Martin were running their T-Birds hard for the title, Jeff Gordon (number 24) conservatively cruised his Chevrolet to the finish for NASCAR's Winston Cup championship.

Alan Kulwicki made it five in 1992, the same year Ford copped its first manufacturer's title. Thunderbirds were dominant from the start, winning the 1992 season's first nine races—four in a row by Elliott. A more consistent Kulwicki (he had but two wins) finished only 10 points ahead of Awesome Bill for the driver's title in the closest championship run to date.

Thunderbird dominance resurfaced in 1994 as Ford pilots captured 20 races, with Pontiac refugee Rusty Wallace taking home eight trophies in his new T-Bird. Mark Martin scored half of Ford's eight wins in 1995, one of which was Dale Jarrett's first for Robert Yates Racing.

Jarrett's Thunderbird roared to a third-place finish in 1996 Winston Cup seasonal points. Then he and Martin ran

hard all year at the top in 1997, eventually falling just short. Needing an eighteenth-place finish at the season-ending NAPA 500 in Atlanta to clinch the championship, Chevrolet driver Jeff Gordon cruised to seventeenth place, while Jarrett and Martin battled to second and third, respectively, behind Bobby Labonte's winning Pontiac. Gordon captured his third Winston Cup title in three years with 4,710 points. Jarrett was second with 4,696, and Martin third at 4,681. It was NASCAR's fourth closest victory margin, and the tightest ever measured from first to third.

It was also a suitably dramatic send-off for Ford's NASCAR Thunderbird, as high-flying a competitor as stock-car racing has ever seen.

Index